Reflecting with God

Reflecting with God

*Connecting Faith and Daily Life
in Small Groups*

ABIGAIL JOHNSON

THE
ALBAN
INSTITUTE

Herndon, Virginia
www.alban.org

Library of Congress Cataloging-in-Publication Data

Johnson, Abigail.
    Reflecting with God : connecting faith and daily life in small groups / Abigail Johnson.
        p. cm.
    Includes bibliographical references.
    ISBN 1-56699-292-3
    1. Church group work. 2. Small groups—Religious aspects—Christianity. 3. Christian life. I. Title.
    BV652.2.J63 2004
    253'.7—dc22

08   07   06   05   04   VG   1   2   3   4   5   6   7   8   9   10

Contents

Foreword

FOR MANY YEARS, AS A SEMINARY DIRECTOR of field education, I supervised theological students in diverse field education settings. Part of our process involved regular reflection on their experience of ministry. In addition, as a spiritual director and a teacher of spiritual formation, I meet regularly with laity and clergy who have invited me to journey with them as spiritual guide. In these settings, whether in field education seminars, classes in spirituality, retreats, or spiritual direction sessions, theological reflection on life experience was and is an essential element of our encounter. Often, however, those with whom I meet resist or are unable to engage in theological reflection. They are instantly willing to consider the psychological, social, political, and cultural dimensions of reality, but they remain shy about reflecting on faith questions.

Recently a clergy friend told me of her experience leading a training event with church members on the church's response to the continuing crisis in the Middle East. After hearing a report on the grave difficulties faced by Palestinians living in East Jerusalem, participants began to focus on the political and social issues. Whenever my friend tried to steer the discussion in a theological direction by raising questions such as "Where do we sense the presence of God in this situation?" the group responded with awkward silence—and soon turned again to discussing the political and sociological dimensions of the problem.

We need Abigail Johnson's book! Her timely and wise work encourages all of us to claim our calling as theologians. This experienced pastor and educator affirms and highlights the essential ministry of the laity in daily life. Her definition of "a theologian [as] someone who intentionally reflects on his or her faith in light of the biblical story and tries to live that faith in daily life" succinctly summarizes the basis of her book. Further, Johnson asserts, "not only can we theologically reflect, but as faithful people of God, we *must* theologically reflect to keep our faith lively and relevant." Beginning with these affirmations, Johnson demonstrates that theological reflection was an essential element in the story of Jesus and has been central to the church's story through the ages.

But how do we, today, help one another engage in regular, lively theological reflection? Relating stories of parishioners who seek to connect their lived experience with their faith, Johnson invites us into vibrant listening. The author's list of excellent questions offers provocative grist for our reflective practice:

> Where is God in this situation? Where is God for others?
> What biblical stories or images come to mind?
> What theological themes come to mind?
> What church traditions connect with this event?

These are a few of the many questions she recommends to assist our individual and group reflection.

Johnson also provides ample guidance for both group facilitators and participants. Chapters three and four identify specific guidelines and models for engaging in theological reflection with a group and as individuals. The role of the facilitator, methods for inviting participation, setting a schedule, the location of sessions, and an outline for meetings are addressed with thoroughness, clarity, and creativity.

Johnson also outlines how group members can write about a life situation for presentation to a group—the starting point for the group's reflection. She recommends seven significant steps—the first six of which begin with pertinent and evocative questions. An individual describes a particular experience to present to the theological reflection group, first exploring his or her feelings about the experience and then thoughts about the social, power, and economic issues present in the experience. Here is where the experience I, and others, have had with theological reflection comes into play: sharing one's thoughts on social, political, and cultural issues is encouraged. Only after these reflections does the writer/presenter move to faith connections. Finally, as the presenter considers what he or she has learned from the entire process, he or she prays, giving thanks for awareness and insight that have arisen and offering up the entire reflection to God.

After a written presentation has been prepared, the theological reflection group, which has created a group covenant, meets to listen carefully and prayerfully and then to respond to the presenter. Johnson is very clear that "the group discussion is not an opportunity to solve the presented problem or psychologize about what is happening in a person's life." The group process is about making faith connections, raising questions, being aware of necessary ambiguity, and specifically *not* about solving the presenter's problems.

Particularly helpful for the new facilitator is Johnson's discussion of circumstances that are difficult in reflection groups, "wrinkles in the fabric." She thoroughly and directly confronts areas such as discomfort with silence, conflicts regarding styles and values among participants, and group members who dominate or who try to persuade others of their dearly held "truths."

"Outward Ripples," Johnson's last chapter, takes us beyond the specific group reflection to ways this process enhances the life of a congregation and the wider community. Worship in its various corporate manifestations can be transformed through laity and clergy engaged together in theological re-flection. Christian education among children, youth, and adults is strengthened when adults and youth participate in theologi-cal reflection groups. Mutual care for and understanding of one another in a congregation grows exponentially through such groups. The daily work life, family life, and community life of the "whole people of God" deepen and expand through congregants continually asking the question "Where is God in all of this?"

I appreciated Abigail Johnson's use of evocative images and analogies for life-enhancing theological reflection. Jazz impro-visation, weaving a tapestry, the ripples stones make when they are tossed into a body of water, musicians' need to regularly practice on their instruments—such images illuminate the spiri-tual process of "reflecting with God." Throughout, Abigail Johnson offers her own life experiences as a pastor, a family member, a violinist, an educator, a Christian on pilgrimage who has discovered for herself the essential necessity and gift of theological reflection.

The last sentences of chapter four might well be the final sentences of the entire book: "The process of reflection is a conversation with God rather than an exercise to complete.... I invite you to begin the reflection process. God waits breath-lessly!"

May we continue the conversation to which Abigail Johnson convincingly invites us.

Barbara B. Troxell
Retired United Methodist clergywoman
Senior Scholar in Spiritual Formation
Garrett-Evangelical Theological Seminary

Preface

OUR MOST CHALLENGING TASK AS FAITHFUL CHRISTIANS is to discern how God is at work in our lives. Through our faith in God as creator and sustainer, we profess our belief that God is part of the fabric of our being, yet naming how God plays that part is difficult. In everyday tasks, decisions, and life challenges, it is not easy to see God's spirit at work.

As a minister of a congregation, I enjoyed opportunities for many conversations with people as they tried to discern and follow God's leading spirit. Joel,* a young man heading off to university, prayerfully considered his career choice. Nancy wrestled with a diagnosis of skin cancer and asked why God had let this happen to her. Bill had been laid off from work and wondered what God was saying to him. Was this an opportunity for new directions or punishment for an unfocused life? Jenny and Matthew faced the dissolution of their marriage; they felt perplexed about the vows they had made to God before the whole congregation. Sadie, at 92 years old, sat for long days in a nursing home, wondering what her life was all about at such a great age. In these conversations, I offered

---

* These examples in the preface are composite situations, with characters whose names are fictional.

pastoral assurance that God is a loving presence in all our lives. It became clear to me, as I talked with folk on their journey with God, that people wanted to know not simply that God *was with them*; they wanted to talk about *how* God was with them.

From these many conversations, I realized that few opportunities are available for people in congregations to gather and reflect together on the connections between their daily lives and their life of faith. In few places are the people of God invited to ask pressing questions of life and faith: *How does God connect to my life? How does my faith inform my decisions? How can I interpret events through the lens of my beliefs?* To explore these questions, I gathered small groups of people to talk with one another through theological reflection. Such reflection offers a structure for talking about what is happening in people's lives, while encouraging a deeper connection to God.

In addition, I have used theological reflection in congregational work and at the theological college where I now work with field-education students. My experience indicates that participants in these groups appreciate a chance to talk about what is going on in their lives and to be heard by others. Group discussion raises wonderful reflection on God's creative spirit and offers room to explore perplexing questions about that spirit at work. Life and energy, laughter and tears, joy and sadness, shared concerns and prayers—all these are offered. In this small group, this small faith community, participants renew their sense of the immediacy of God's loving spirit and find companions on their spiritual journey.

From the joy of working with many groups, I wanted to offer this process to other congregations that are seeking ways to help members and friends find a greater connection between faith and life. Other authors have also recognized this need for theological reflection, and you will see their books listed in the bibliography. But in this book, you will find a step-by-step, hands-on approach, outlining formation of groups, suggestions for group facilitators, and clear instruction for doing theological reflection. Whether you are an experienced group leader or a new facilitator, you can put a group together and begin guiding the process of theological reflection with the instructions offered here.

Acknowledgments

The work of putting this book together has taken many years, and I have received input from hundreds of group participants, each one remembered and treasured. John and B. J. Klassen have been mentors through living their lives authentically and courageously. Family members have offered support that has pushed me beyond the limits of what I could imagine. Beth Gaede, editor, has offered me feedback and many suggestions to help me communicate a tangle of ideas more clearly. Her enthusiasm for this project is greatly appreciated. All these voices and many more have created an offering that I hope will be useful to you and to other faithful people who desire to hear God's voice and feel God's presence nearly and clearly.

1

A Call to Be Faithful

SHEILA, A NURSE IN A BUSY DOWNTOWN HOSPITAL, feels the stress of financial cutbacks in her workplace that make it difficult for her to give enough attention to each patient.* A faithful member of her local congregation, she often wonders how God's spirit is at work in the various dimensions of health care. Although her time at worship on Sunday morning offers her spiritual renewal to continue her demanding work, she nonetheless feels a "disconnect" between her faith and her work in the hospital. Talking about her faith at work in what is considered a secular context is not appropriate, yet when dealing with life-and-death issues as well as the matter of what it means to be healthy, Sheila finds questions bubbling up within her. The faith questions that arise in the workplace seem out of place at church because they cannot be easily addressed within the congregation's committee structure or adult-education programs.

Likewise, Connor, a dedicated teacher, tries to connect his love of God with his love of teaching. Working with students from a variety of backgrounds, he realizes that teaching is more

* These are composite stories and fictional characters drawn from real-life situations.

1

than simply dealing with the content of mathematics, reading, and social science. Teaching encompasses the lives of his students. He knows that if they are struggling with issues at home, they cannot concentrate at school. He has often thought of setting up a breakfast program to address the needs of students who arrive at school hungry. He knows that his congregation is interested in outreach projects, but he isn't sure how such a program might connect to his work at school.

Dale finds himself in a similar situation. Having recently moved into the area, he and his family are interested in transferring their membership from their previous congregation. Dale works for the government in the area of affordable housing. While his wife, Cindy, is interested in helping with the church school, and his children are becoming active in various children's programs, Dale wonders how he might get involved in congregational life. The chair of the board suggested that Dale might help by washing the communion cups after worship, since the member who used to do that job is no longer available. While he is happy to wash communion cups, Dale somehow feels that his full resources are not being used by the congregation. He wonders how he might connect his affordable-housing work with his congregational commitment.

Lucy, a recent mother, has made a transition from the hurly-burly of a corporate position in business to the topsy-turvy pace of looking after an infant. She has joined a mother's group at the church where all the moms have an opportunity to exchange stories about the challenges of broken sleep, teething problems, diaper rash, and balancing time for family and self. Lucy appreciates the conversation in the group but still feels a need to reflect on her recent experiences at a deeper level. While she is totally overwhelmed with gratitude and awe at the birth of her baby, she is equally overwhelmed by the tedium of day-to-day motherhood. She misses her busy and demanding workplace, yet she treasures time with her new daughter. Feeling a new spiritual awareness of creation but also feeling close to tears with weariness and her new identity, Lucy craves a place to talk about her experiences in light of a shift in her faith. She views the world differently now with the birth of her daughter and wishes she had someone to talk to.

All these people have something in common. They want to connect the issues and situations in their daily life with their inner life of faith. What they are feeling is a rift between their daily activities and their sense of where God is at work. They are faithful church members, contributing to its life and work, yet a gap separates church life from daily life for them. The words of faith on Sunday morning have great meaning but are difficult to transfer to the daily decisions to be made through the week. These people are asking: "How do we connect our daily life with our faith?"

Making Connections

Untangling the day-to-day issues in our lives can seem daunting. We lead multifaceted lives. As parents, we support our children through various stages of their lives, knowing that the world they inhabit is different from the world in which we grew up. In a changing world, we suffer stress in the workplace from trying to stay current and competitive; moreover, we must deal with financial and workforce cutbacks. In addition, we try to balance our work life with a commitment to spend "quality" time with family and friends. We want to have a comfortable lifestyle, but at the same time we want to be good stewards of our time, talents, and resources. Amid these concerns, we need to do the laundry, buy groceries, cook meals, and keep the house in order. Time to sit quietly and reflect is rare. We may have good intentions to reflect on the many layers of our lives, but the busyness of our existence tends to take priority over quiet time. Typically we reflect on issues by letting them rattle around in our heads. If we are fortunate, we have good friends or close family members with whom to talk things through and find some clarity, but at many times we feel isolated and lonely.

As people of faith, we add another layer to our reflections by wondering where God fits into our lives. A popular way of addressing this layer has been "WWJD," the initials for "What would Jesus do?" People have worn bracelets with this insignia as a helpful reminder to look at life through the lens of Jesus' life and ministry. I found that while this bracelet was helpful for a while, it was soon forgotten or discarded among other items on a bedroom dresser, or tucked away in a drawer. Aside from a general sense of what Jesus might do in particular 21st-century situations, we need a clear and deliberate process for thinking through our experiences—a process that enables us to look at life through the lens of faith to connect all our life to God. I believe that God's Spirit is at work in the tasks we do and the decisions we make. God joins us in the nitty-gritty of our lives. Whether we are dealing with routines or handling crises, God's presence strengthens us and gives us clarity and focus. That's where theological reflection fits in.

In a broad sense, theological reflection happens any time that we wonder about God, our faith, our beliefs, and our values. We reflect theologically when we pray, and in the midst of crisis when we ask, "Why me, God?" We do it when we ask, "Is that all there is?" We do it when we try to bring justice into the decisions we make. Although such theological reflection takes place, it can often be random and unstructured. In this book, I offer a structured process for engaging in theological reflection by looking at a situation or event through a series of questions. These questions are designed to help individuals and small groups think through situations with the eyes of faith. A more detailed description is offered in chapter 4. Through this process, Sheila, Connor, Dale, and Lucy had an opportunity to meet together as a group with two other members of their congregation to reflect on current situations in their lives. They found it helpful to get to know one another more deeply, to think through specific issues, and to talk about how these issues connected to their faith. An enriching experience, it profoundly affected for each of them the life of faith. They began to see that their lives belonged to God, that everything that they did and said was connected to God.

Belonging to God

Belonging to God is an ancient concept. Biblical stories tell us in various ways that we belong to God through creation, connection, and call. In the opening chapters of Genesis we read the account of how God created the universe and began a close, intimate relationship with all creation. In forming humanity in the divine image, God made a special connection that draws us into personal relationship. Within that relationship, God calls us to be stewards of the earth in partnership with one another, carrying out an active ministry of care for creation and all living beings. Through creation, connection, and call, we belong to God.

We hear this message of belonging again and again. In the poetic language of the psalmist, we hear that God knew us in our very creation, before we were born, in the knitting of our bones in our mother's womb (Psalm 139). God's connection to us is intimate because our Creator knows our very thoughts. To be in such an intimate relationship with God is profoundly moving, yet somehow we have lost that deep sense of connection to God. We use the word *secular* to describe a world outside divine sacredness, as if it were possible to separate God from creation. In renewing our understanding of God's presence within all creation, we can hear the Creator's call to us more clearly.

Throughout the Old Testament and the New Testament, biblical stories describe God's calling us to offer our lives in service. Jesus went into the countryside and walked beside lakes, calling a few to join him in preaching, teaching, and proclaiming

God's love for humanity. Yet Jesus calls everyone into a deeper relationship with God and one another. Speaking to the crowds that gathered to hear his words, using stories from everyday life, Jesus spoke of God's call to justice and right relationship with one another. In a sense, he reflected theologically on ordinary situations and events in people's lives as instances in which God's word of love can be lived. In this way, Jesus calls us all to life in abundance.

Perhaps we regard God's call as being only for special people, for those who consider themselves set aside to serve God as ordained ministers. Perhaps it is hard to believe that God would have an interest in the daily aspects of our ordinary lives. Yet the reality is that God has a deep knowledge of and interest in each of us, calling forth our unique and distinct gifts for ministry within the lives we lead.

Within our church traditions, such terms as "the whole people of God" or "the priesthood of all believers" have been used in an attempt to lift up the lives of laity. In our churches, we have good intentions to value the gifts and ministry of laity. The reality is that ministry is usually seen as the work of ordained ministers, while laypeople assist that ministry through serving on Christian education committees or congregational boards, or by reading Scripture in worship. Although this kind of service to the church is valuable, the life of laity that exists outside the church walls rarely comes into focus in congregational life.

It is easy to see that clergy are serving God and that everything they do belongs explicitly to God. It is much harder to see what it means for laity to belong to God. We have been created to be in connection with God. From this connection, we are called to offer all our lives in service to God and one another. Although we may believe such a concept, making that belief concrete in our day-to-day activities is hard. Does God have a part in deciding whether we use cloth or disposable diapers? Does it matter to God what kinds of books a teacher chooses for a curriculum? Is God interested in how statistical analysis is used in computer applications? I believe that God is intensely involved in all these aspects of our lives. What we need is a way to awaken our sense of God's presence and connection to our lives.

Belonging to God is both a personal and a communal experience, because we are called into relationship with God and with one another. If bringing my daily life to church is important, then it is equally important to know about the daily lives of others. Typically, we know very little about one another outside our interactions on church committees. At a recent workshop on the ministry of the laity, I asked people to do a little exercise that you might enjoy engaging in right now. Write down the names of 10 people you know at church. Beside their names, answer the following questions:

- What kind of work do they do?
- In what areas of their life do they find satisfaction?
- What are their struggles?
- What are their gifts for ministry? Do they recognize their gifts?
- Would they use the word *ministry* to describe what they do? If yes, why? If no, why not?
- How might you enable them to claim their gifts for ministry?

When doing this exercise, you may be able to answer all these questions in great detail. Yet typically, I find that people can answer the first question a little and the following questions hardly at all. Not only do we not have a sense of belonging to God; we do not have a sense of belonging to one another. While making deeper connections to one another is not necessary for theological reflection, it does add enrichment. If we take seriously our sense of being part of the body of Christ, then we may have need of one another as we discern how God works in our lives.

To sum up: We can claim a sense of belonging to God through reflecting on our lives and perhaps reflecting together with others. We belong to God through our creation by God, through our intimate connection to God, and in our call from God. In responding to God's call, we celebrate that we belong to God and God belongs to us.

The Ministry of Our Lives

I assume that God calls all of us into relationship through our baptism and membership in the body of Christ, and that we respond to God's call by offering our lives in service to God and to one another. Saying that in a grand sweeping gesture is one thing, but living as if we believe it is another. Let us go back to the four individuals who opened the chapter.

Sheila works in an intensive-care unit. She sees many people come and go in crises of one sort or another. Several times she has called the hospital chaplain to attend to families in distress, as hospital protocol does not give her the time or a mandate to offer spiritual care. She feels that she has her job to do, and that someone else can minister to the patient's or family's spiritual needs. However, through theological reflection with a small group, she has begun to shift her thinking to realize that she too has a ministry to offer. While she offers something different from the chaplain, nonetheless her work as a nurse is a powerful ministry. Through her sensitivity and efficient routine, people feel calmer even in the midst of pain. Sheila takes time to give clear descriptions of what medical procedures she is administering so that people under her care know what is going on and why. Sheila's whole sense of her work changes when she begins to see that with her hands she offers God's love and care. Because of her calm words and careful attention to medical procedures, God's healing spirit is at work in her patients' lives. This emerging sense of her ministry enables her to discuss, through the lens of faith, the more complex issues that arise at work.

As a teacher, Connor was obliged only to teach the curriculum for grade five and to go home at the end of the day. However, Connor felt a restlessness that he needed to do more. He was not simply teaching a subject or offering course content. He was in relationship with a whole person, a growing child in his care. Through reflecting theologically, he began to understand this restlessness as God's call, an intuition to reach beyond the basics of his teaching and to offer more to his students. Through encouragement from his theological reflection group, Connor approached the church's outreach committee. He was surprised and pleased that committee members received his idea of a breakfast program with enthusiasm. Even more surprisingly, they asked how they could help him. He had imagined that he was simply delivering a good idea to people who would take over and run everything. Now he realized that they were ready to assist *him* in realizing *his* call to this ministry. With some initial work, this project became a reality in his school, as well as in several other schools, under the care of hundreds of volunteers. By enacting his vision of ministry, school and community came together to meet the needs of disadvantaged children.

Dale was interested in joining the theological reflection group because he saw it as a good opportunity to talk about his work. Passionate about the concept of affordable housing for all, he often felt tied up in bureaucratic red tape and seldom was able to follow his dream. He thought he would talk about work, but he ended up talking about God and his deep desire to feel in relationship with God, not as an interesting idea but as a deeply felt connection. What moved Dale into this sense of relationship was having a small group of people praying for him. They prayed with him as he wrestled with ethical decisions at his workplace. When he was at meetings during his work time, he knew that members of the group were praying for him as he took stands on significant issues. He grew to understand through the connection with group members that God was with him. His work was not simply a matter of social justice; it was a vital ministry to God's people.

A gregarious person, Lucy had no trouble chatting with people, but whenever she began to talk about the birth of her baby, tears welled up and she became speechless. In the theological reflection group she began to find words to describe the deep sense of awe she felt at having given birth. Having brought life into the world, she felt a connection to all of life. In the miracle of birth, she felt gratitude for the gift of new life and wanted to find ways to give thanks. Within the group, she began to offer those thanks to God and felt released to express an emerging spirituality that she had not previously realized within herself. This new awareness helped to sustain her through long nights when her baby was teething. Her sense of feeling close to God and creation gave her a new identity far broader than the identity she had had within the workplace. Although she planned to resume her career at some point, she felt a different perspective toward her workplace, not as the prime focus of her life but as a part of a larger picture of creation.

Through the process of theological reflection, Sheila, Connor, Dale, and Lucy all found a deeper awareness of God's presence in their lives and a renewed sense of God's call.

Our Gifts for Ministry

If God calls us—each and every one of us—to offer ourselves in service to the world through the daily events of our lives, then it follows that we all have gifts for ministry, because God wouldn't call us to something for which we are not equipped. However, most people feel shy about naming their gifts. Culturally we have been raised not to put ourselves forward or "puff ourselves up." Yet I suggest that naming our gifts is a question of self-awareness, not of self-aggrandizement or self-absorption.

Let's go back to our sense of belonging to God. In Genesis, we see God engaged in the heavy work of creation. At various stages along the way, God stops and looks around and proclaims that what has been created is good. God has no hesitation in naming the gift of creativity and in declaring the outcome good. Over and over again, God sees that various aspects of creation are good. God has a gift for creating; and in relationship with God, we give thanks and praise for God's gifts. In creating humanity, God called us to be fruitful and multiply, to be careful stewards of this creation. In worship, we give thanks for the bounty of the earth and for those people who contribute to the fruitfulness of creation through their special gifts. And that giftedness includes us.

In Psalm 139, our closeness to God is described as deep and intimate. God is present everywhere, from heaven to hell, in night and day, in joy and despair. From formation in the womb to a lifelong relationship, God is present. God's hand will lead us and hold us fast and safe. Whether we are on the mountaintop of joy or in the depths of hell, God maintains a steadfast presence. God has created us and blessed us to serve in furthering creation. Can we really serve this God by denying gifts and abilities that have been so freely bestowed upon us? We do not serve God well by pretending that we do not have gifts. We do not serve one another well by being self-effacing and refusing to offer our gifts and abilities. These gifts have been given to us so that we may fulfill our vocation as people of God. In the very stuff of our lives, God is present and attentive to our vocation and our needs.

Often the challenge for us is to identify our gifts. In a general sense, we serve God in everything we do and in everything we say. In our daily relationships with family members and co-workers, we try to live the love of God. We try to make informed and just decisions in whatever situations arise. Yet God may call us to serve in a particular way with particular gifts. For instance, Joellen named her sense of call as "wanting to make a difference in people's lives." She became a social worker and worked in a variety of settings where she gained experience and learned a great deal. Over the years, she saw a common thread in her work with people and a special gift she had to offer. She began to see that anger was often at the heart of many destructive behaviors and that she had an ability to address that anger. Through study and experimental group workshops on anger, she began to see people turn their lives around in positive ways. Through a process of theological reflection she was able to give voice to her hunches and find courage to move in different directions. Recently, judges have begun to recognize her anger-management program as helpful, recommending it as an alternative to incarceration. From a general sense of wanting to make a difference, she moved to clarity about how her special gifts would make that difference.

Our specific gifts may be offered in the very tasks that we do in our daily work. For instance, one person may have the gift of teaching and give expression to that gift through teaching youngsters in a school setting. Another may have a prophetic voice and exercise it through working in the forefront of the environmental movement. However, our gifts may not be best expressed in our workplace. A career that gives us a clear sense of serving God with the best that we have to offer is a wonderful privilege. Not everyone has that privilege. Many people must find ways to serve God other than in paid employment. Sometimes people are able to exercise their spiritual gifts, those gifts that bring deep satisfaction, through work in the community, within their family life, or within the church. For instance, in the past many women found themselves exercising gifts of leadership through women's groups in the church at a time when they were not able to, or did not wish to, work outside the home. As a leader of a congregation, I am grateful for this ministry.

Mabel, a quiet and gentle person now in her late 70s, leads the team that prepares and serves funeral lunches or teas. Ready at a moment's notice, Mabel will arrive at the church with her baskets of supplies to provide sandwiches, desserts, and beverages for families in grief and distress. She pays attention to details that provide a warm, welcoming atmosphere with special flowers, tablecloths, chairs arranged in small conversational groupings. Mabel is too shy actually to speak to the people who are so grief-stricken, yet she offers comfort through providing space for the bereaved to meet, to share stories of a loved one, and to be fed in body and spirit. Mabel loves this work and derives tremendous satisfaction from her unsung ministry.

Rather than get involved in church activities, however, many people throw themselves into community life through volunteering with service clubs, coaching sports groups, or working with an environmental agency. We may need to use our gifts in a variety of places to find a sense of serving God and responding to our call. Some of the resources available to help us identify our spiritual gifts are listed in the bibliography. They help the reader find language to speak of spiritual gifts, offering a useful framework to think about how to respond to God's call.

However, an opportunity to talk about the activities in which we find greatest satisfaction or feel a sense of restlessness and a desire to do more—an opportunity such as a theological reflection group—can bring to the surface an even greater sense of our ministry. Taking time to talk with one another and sharing with people who will listen deeply can show us how God is at work in our lives and what special gifts we have to serve God. Others who see us as unique and gifted individuals may affirm abilities that we see as ordinary. Our confidence in naming our gifts can be encouraged by our faith community through a small group of people willing to journey with us.

An Invitation

At this point, I invite you to consider trying a process of theological reflection. The following chapters will give clear, usable guidelines for getting started and engaging in this venture.

Whether you do it as a personal journey, or through a small-group gathering, I encourage you to enter into a season of thinking through the lens of faith about the situations and events of your life. Through reflecting theologically, we deepen a sense of belonging to God. We hear God's call to us and begin to discern how we can respond to that call. We discover our spiritual gifts and understand what it means to share in Christ's ministry. God is calling. Let us respond.

2

An Ancient and Ever-Unfolding Story

"I'M NOT A THEOLOGIAN!" That was Mary's response when I suggested to her Bible study group that we are all theologians. This group of laypeople had been meeting with one another for almost 22 years, reflecting on Scripture, reading the latest book on the Bible and faith. They read church study documents and often had clear and strong views on church doctrine and their own faith. As a facilitator of this group, I enjoyed the stimulating and challenging discussion. Yet they were alarmed when I suggested that they were all theologians. Of course, none of them were theologians, if that meant years of formal theological education or a doctorate in theology. By such a definition, very few people are theologians. However, my definition is rooted in an understanding of the ministry of the laity. A theologian is someone who intentionally reflects on his or her faith in light of the biblical story and tries to live that faith in daily life. It had never occurred to them that they were theologians. Once the idea was introduced, they felt they had permission to entertain the possibility that they were indeed theologians. As they talked, they began to grow in confidence, professing that title for themselves. They realized that they were laying claim to their baptismal call to ministry.

Several months later, having read a challenging book by a biblical scholar, they summoned up their courage to invite this scholar to meet with them for discussion of his book. What followed was a lively discussion in which they asked questions and cleared up areas of confusion. Toward the end of the meeting, one venerable group member, Sarah, asked the scholar if he would like some feedback on his book. He said yes. Sarah praised his interesting ideas but suggested that he could write more clearly. The scholar's reaction was surprise. He responded, "I didn't write this book for laypeople. I wrote it for biblical scholars." Sarah told him, "I am a biblical scholar, too."

A seed of an idea planted many months before—that these group members were theologians—had germinated and come to full bloom. They were beginning to understand that while they did not have formal theological education, the years of dedicated reading, research, and weekly discussion as faithful Christians meant that they could lay claim to theological and biblical wisdom. Often laypeople do not feel confident in their ability to think theologically. Our church structures and academic hierarchy tend to undermine confidence. However, not only do I believe that all faithful Christians are theologians; I believe that we are all called to be theologians, leading active, reflective lives of faith. Not only *can* we reflect theologically, but also as faithful people of God we *must* do so to keep our faith lively and relevant.

Most people do not have the opportunity for intensive weekly Bible study. Nonetheless, all of us can take a little time in our week for prayer and theological reflection. In addition, being part of a reflection group or talking with a spiritual mentor from time to time offers further enrichment through the exchange of ideas and challenges to our assumptions. We are not alone in this process of prayer and theological reflection, because we have a vast and ancient Judeo-Christian heritage behind us, as well as a faith community that travels alongside us. In addition, God's spirit is threaded throughout these ancient and present-day stories, beckoning us toward future horizons.

Being faithful and reflective, being theologians, is part of an ancient story set out in the Bible, a story that has been unfolding for centuries in the church. We join that continuing story, adding stories from our own faith lives. Yet my invitation for us to be reflective, faithful theologians is important not only for Christians today. My hope is that God's people will continually respond to that invitation as our living stories unfold. Theological reflection grows out of our biblical heritage and has been nurtured throughout our theological history. Now it is our turn to become part of that ever-unfolding story.

The Story and Our Story

As mentioned earlier, a theologian is someone who intentionally reflects on his or her faith in light of the biblical story and tries to live that faith in daily life. Theological reflection is that point where the biblical story and our story intersect.

As Christians, we look to the Bible, in particular to the stories of Jesus, as a source of faith and inspiration. Jesus was a theologian. He reflected on his experiences in light of Jewish scriptures, in light of synagogue tradition, in conversation with his disciples, in response to challenges by the community, and in prayer with God. His faith was clear and deep, yet open and fluid.

Early in his ministry, Jesus took time in the desert to pray and reflect on Scripture. For Jesus, Scripture meant a collection of writings called the law, the prophets, and wisdom literature. When tempted by Satan, Jesus was able to draw on Scripture to respond to his adversary. His responses confirmed his deep relationship with God and clarified his call to ministry. Jesus began a new ministry, rooted in his love for God—a ministry lived through his itinerant preaching, teaching, and healing.

Yet Jesus was rooted not only in a relationship with God; he related to a particular faith community through the synagogue. During a Sabbath service, we hear Jesus refer to himself as a fulfillment of Scripture, as one who will faithfully live God's call to free the captives, bring sight to the blind, and heal the sick. Also, his clear sense of call to ministry framed his critique of those who were more interested in following the minute details of religious law than in addressing the needs of those who were hungry, ill, or poor.

While Jesus attracted many followers through his teaching and healing, he also upset, even offended, others by his approach to ministry. Religious authorities tried to trip Jesus up by posing questions related to religious laws. It was his ability to connect the scriptural story to the story unfolding before him that turned the tables on his questioners. Those without sin could cast the first stone at the adulterer—and, of course, who could claim to be without sin?

In his teaching, Jesus used stories and everyday illustrations to help people reflect theologically. His characters sowed seed, swept floors, and cast nets for fishing—everyday tasks that helped people connect their lives to God. People responded to these stories. Zaccheus reflected on his life and made some dramatic changes, such as ethical tax collecting. The Samaritan woman, surprised by the way Jesus could connect her life story with the larger faith story, became a witness to her people. Some, like Peter and Simon, chose new directions for their lives by following Jesus and exercising their own ministry of teaching and healing. Jesus did not set up barriers to a relationship with God. Rather, he worked hard to remove barriers created by church rules and regulations, social systems, and personal disempowerment. He enabled people to reflect theologically on their lives to see God's Spirit at work.

As well as being able to challenge his faith community, he was open to being challenged. Jesus believed he was called to heal the children of God, those children being his particular faith community. Yet when a woman declared that even the dogs were allowed to eat crumbs from the children's table, Jesus was challenged to rethink his belief. His gifts were not exclusive to one faith community but available to all. Not only could Jesus reflect on life experience in light of Scripture; he could also reflect on Scripture in light of life experience, even when that meant changing previous convictions.

Finally, Jesus' most profound theological reflection came through his prayer life. He regularly took time apart from his teaching and healing to pray, finding a place apart from the crowds to talk with God. We catch a glimpse of the intimacy of his relationship with God through his use of "Daddy," or "Abba," when addressing God. Prayer was part of his ministry life and his decision making. He prayed in the garden of Gethsemane, and struggled to reconcile his obedience to God with his knowledge of the religious, social, and political situation at hand. He knew that following God's call was his death sentence. For Jesus, prayer was not only intimate conversation with God; it was a means of theological reflection, a connection between his faith and his life.

Jesus was able to reflect on the intersection of the Scriptures he knew and his daily life, to reflect on "The Story" and *his* story. In following Jesus, we are called to reflect on our experiences in light of Scripture, in light of our faith tradition, in conversation with others, in response to challenges by our communities, and in prayer with God. Such reflection will give birth to a faith that is clear and deep, yet open and fluid.

A Community's Story

Following the traumatic death of Jesus, his disciples and followers were in disarray. Their beloved leader and hope for the future was dead. But this death was extraordinary, because death was not the final word. People saw Jesus resurrected from the dead. They ate, drank, and talked with Jesus. These astound-

ing experiences of Jesus resurrected gave hope to a fractured
community. As this early Jesus community tried to make sense
of the death and resurrection of their revered leader, they clung
to the sayings and actions of Jesus, telling stories of his life and
ministry. Jesus had promised to return, and his early disciples
were in a state of readiness to welcome him back. Yet as time
went by, his followers needed to learn how to live without him.
Beyond telling the stories, followers of Jesus were trying to
understand what his life, death, and resurrection meant for their
daily life. They were engaged in theological reflection.

In a society where few people were able to read, stories of
Jesus remained part of an oral tradition until time and dispersed communities made it difficult to maintain that core
teaching through oral tradition alone. Writing down the stories of Jesus helped to keep his words alive and offered the
gospel message to other parts of the world for people who
could read. However, different communities developed differ-
ing written accounts, creating or reflecting their own theological understandings of Jesus. The varying accounts raised
questions as to which version had authority.

Who had the authority to say who Jesus was and what his
life, death, and resurrection meant for the ongoing faith community? Initially, close followers of Jesus had that authority.
They had traveled with Jesus, heard his intimate thoughts, and
experienced firsthand his teaching and healing ministries. Later,
those close to the disciples were given that authority for handing down the oral and written stories of Jesus, for maintaining
that tradition. As time went by and as fewer firsthand witnesses
to the Jesus stories were still living, the faith community had
to rely on written resources alone. They needed to reflect on
the Scriptures Jesus knew, as well as on newly written Gospels
and letters.

Even with written accounts of Jesus' life and letters from
church leaders such as Paul, questions arose as to who Jesus
was. In addition, in Jesus' time, many itinerant preachers and

teachers traveled the ancient Mediterranean world. So what was special about Jesus? Understanding Jesus was essential, because it was dangerous to be a follower of Jesus. People were persecuted and put to death for following him, so it was important for people to know *why* Jesus was the man to follow. Lives were at stake. To address these profound concerns, Jesus' followers continued to reflect on their lives in light of their experiences of Jesus. They began to search the same Scriptures that Jesus knew to understand the meaning of Jesus' life and ministry. They came to the conclusion that he was not simply an itinerant preacher but was in fact a direct line to God. He was more than another prophetic messenger from God; he was God's Son. He was God in the flesh. Dying for Jesus meant being obedient to God and joining Jesus in paradise. This was a message of good news that was like no other.

The Church's Story

Jesus reflected on the Scriptures he knew in light of his experiences, and in turn his followers reflected on his teachings and actions, which were later recorded and which have become food for our own reflection on the New Testament. In every generation, people have begun with the faith witness of their forebears, have reflected on that witness, and in turn have provided material on which others can reflect. This is the story of the church, and we become part of that "great cloud of witnesses," adding our stories to the ever-unfolding story. We catch a glimpse of that story in the development of the church.

The transition from a frightened band of Jesus followers to the organized churches of today has taken place over 2,000 years, with succeeding generations addressing the pastoral and community concerns of their time in light of scriptural writing that has emerged since Jesus' death. Early Jesus followers came to be known as "Christ followers," or Christians. Small, dispersed Christian communities chose leaders and teachers, met

regularly to worship, and organized themselves to care for the
sick and the poor. With the acceptance of Christianity by
Constantine as the state religion, Christians enjoyed freedom
from persecution and social stability. Yet this stability was not
reflected within the church community, because the various
Christian communities understood Jesus differently.

Constantine was eager for the church to become a unified,
well-established, stabilizing force in society. To achieve such
stability, however, the church itself needed to come to some
agreement about who Jesus was and what his ministry, death,
and resurrection meant. Although there were significant social
and political reasons for the church to figure out who Jesus
was, the faith community's understanding of Jesus also had an
impact on people's lives and eternal life. No longer were Christians persecuted and put to death for their beliefs. However,
what they believed about Jesus still had an impact on their
salvation—meaning, what would happen to them after death.
Only God could decide whether a person merited eternal life
or eternal damnation. So what was Jesus' relationship to God?

Christians agreed that Jesus was central to salvation, but
the question of how Jesus was involved in salvation was a hotly
debated issue. As people reflected on the life and ministry of
Jesus, some believed he was a supreme creation of God but
fully human. What that meant was that only God could decide
who was saved for eternal life. Following Jesus, as an absolute
example of a faithful and godly life, meant increasing merit for
heaven. If we were good people like Jesus, then God would
welcome us into heaven.

Others believed that Jesus was fully divine and that, while
he participated in human existence, he was removed from all
pain and suffering. As a fully divine being, Jesus was God visit-
ing among us. As God, Jesus could offer his followers salvation
directly. Yet such a Jesus could not have been human; could
not have felt grief at the death of his friend Lazarus; could not
have been moved by the plight of blind, lame, and sick people;

and could not have suffered pain on the cross. So how could this God relate to us, and how could we relate to God? We need a God we can relate to, a personal God with whom to experience intimate relationship.

After long debates and reflection on Scripture by councils of learned church leaders, an agreement was reached: that Jesus is both fully human and fully divine. This approach was finally agreed upon within the church. Being fully human, Jesus was God in the flesh, participating in and understanding our human condition. Being fully divine, Jesus was one with God in offering salvation, deciding on our eternal life. Jesus' life and ministry were the prime example of how to lead a faithful life, because he was God walking among us and living that faithful life.

A Theological Story

Creeds and doctrines, such as those that name Jesus as fully human and fully divine, arose from real pastoral concerns within faith communities—concerns about how to live life and about what happens after life ends. These creeds and doctrines are statements emerging from theological reflection on real life and community situations in conversation with our biblical texts. Over the years, throughout our church history, we have inherited a wonderful tradition of theological reflection as we continually grapple with issues emerging in each period of history. That tradition offers a bedrock of faith for each new generation.

Along with inheriting a bedrock of faith, we also inherit ties that bind us. Our church history is filled with questions and community concerns that challenged previous theological understandings. The Reformation is one example: political and social concerns pushed at the walls of tradition, breaking open new ways of thinking theologically. For instance, heavy church taxation for building projects through the sale of indulgences

placed burdens on faithful people. Martin Luther, a monk, biblical scholar, and teacher, criticized the church for this unjust
taxation as well as for other practices. He felt that church leaders had lax morals, indulging themselves in rich food, wine,
and women, rather than focusing on the pastoral needs of the
people. After reflecting on the concerns of his day from a biblical basis, he challenged the church to engage in discussion on
95 points of church practice and theology. This challenge ig-
nited years of discussion leading to the establishment of the
Protestant church we know today, as well as a reformation within
the Roman Catholic Church. Thus we inherit not only a bedrock of faith, but also a heritage of protesting and critiquing
for renewal and reform from within our tradition. Again, we
reflect theologically on our personal and communal concerns
in light of Scripture, and the result is a renewed faith.

Theological reflection continues. In more recent history,
liberation theology, with its emphasis on God's "preferential
option for the poor," has challenged traditional theological
thinking, as well as the faith of all those who are economically
privileged. Liberation theology arose from real issues of poverty in Latin America and South America; it reframes our understanding of social justice in North America. Through the
eyes of the poor and with the call of God for political and
economic justice, many have changed their ways of looking at
the world. Feminist theology is an example of theological reflection that has led to a new awareness of female voices in the
social, political, and theological landscape. The voices of women
have broken open theological and church structures, unset-
tling previous assumptions, offering more diverse images of
God and a richer heritage of historical and theological perspectives.

From these examples, we can see that in the past 100 years,
numerous contextual theologies—theologies arising from particular personal and social concerns—have challenged theological traditions. Theology is alive and lively because it is a

conversation arising from real-life situations. We add the stories of our lives to the ongoing story of church history and theology.

In our theological reflection we follow Jesus, who is theological reflector par excellence. We join the disciples and the great cloud of witnesses who have gone before us, people who lived faithfully within their lifetime, who reflected theologically on lively issues and situations. The story of faith in our church history becomes *our* story as we continue the tradition of theological reflection as an ongoing expression of faithful living.

Our Story

Whether we are aware of it or not, we all reflect. Thoughts and images tumble around in our minds as we go over conversations with friends, work issues, and family relationships. Most of the time, our reflection is unconscious, helping us to put our world in order. Our dreams are another form of unconscious reflection, a time to sort through the day's events. Yet not all our reflection is unconscious. At times we need to deal with situations and issues that demand attention. Usually what stands out is an event that touches our feelings or unsettles our ways of thinking. Whenever I have an argument with my sister, I am upset. My feelings of anger, frustration, and hurt come bubbling up. Our long history together and all past hurts, as well as joys, come to the forefront. And I try to think about what to do next. An argument forces me to reflect.

In addition, at times we must deal with traumatic situations, crisis, and tragedy that pull the rug out from under us and leave us questioning our whole lives. For instance, a friend's house was burglarized. After the initial shock and sense of violation, she realized that her long-held belief in the essential goodness of people was shaken. As she thought through her feelings about the burglary, she was challenged to change her assumptions about people's goodness. Although she knew that some people do not respect property and boundaries, she had to learn to trust people again. She was engaged in reflection.

Always Reflecting

While we reflect automatically as we sort and sift through events, more conscious reflection requires us to learn skills and to employ a clear process. Reflection is hard work, and we are not always very good at it. Many people are not able to name feelings or to think clearly about the dynamics of a situation, or to make connections between our story and the biblical story.

We pick up skills for reflection unconsciously as we go through life, as well as those skills that are consciously learned or developed. When I was a child, my mother taught me to count to 10 before exploding in anger. I learned to take time to reflect before I spoke—a skill I am continually learning. Also, in learning how to get along with others as a society, we have had to think about previous ways of doing things and to come up with new ways. For example, in the early days of cars, there was no need for road-safety regulations. As the number of cars on the road and accident rates increased, rules were enacted to ensure that roads would be safe. Thus, reflection on particular situations inspires us to develop new ways of doing things.

In our professions, we inherit traditional ways of doing things, tried-and-true methods. Yet as circumstances change, we must be able to reflect on what is taking place and develop new methods and even new directions. Recently Eastman Kodak, a longtime leader in the manufacture of photographic equipment and supplies, has experienced a downturn in its productivity because of increased sales of digital cameras. People do not need as much film in an increasingly digital world. Thus company officials are reflecting on shifts and changes in business as Kodak adapts to a changing marketplace. Whether in medicine, teaching, law, or engineering, reflection on practice brings innovation. Nonetheless, there will always be tension between what has been done before and the desire or necessity for new frontiers.

Whether our reflection is unconscious or conscious, part of our personal life or our professional life, we Christians bring another perspective to our reflection. God calls us to faithful living expressed through our actions, our beliefs, our study of the Bible and church doctrines and documents, our prayers, and our conversations with our faith community. Also, we immediately have a partner in this reflection: God. As the creedal statement of the United Church of Canada begins, "We are not alone. We live in God's world." We have been created by God, claimed in love by God, called by God, and made accountable to God. We can be certain that we are never separated from the love of God and remain accountable to God, from whom we can never hide and who is steadfast in love. Reflecting theologically sharpens our awareness of the presence of God, drawing us into an ever-closer relationship.

Language for Reflection

Our tradition gives us language for theological reflection. As we reflect on events in our lives, we have a long tradition of biblical stories and insights from our historical faith community, covering the gamut of human situations. The Bible is not an answer book, but it does give us stories about others who struggled to be faithful. While biblical and church heritage may not help us deal with every aspect of contemporary life, our human condition and human reactions to events are recorded in biblical and church tradition. Sin and evil, forgiveness and redemption and reconciliation, joy and despair, transfiguration and abandonment—all are part of the ongoing history of human faithfulness. We can see our story resonating in the stories of those who have gone before us. We are not alone.

Biblical language is rich in theological language useful for theological reflection. The Psalms give us wonderful language to praise God and to rail against injustice. Large narratives such

as the exodus story offer images and metaphors that have caught
the imagination of many oppressed communities, giving them
hope and a call to action. Gospel stories become part of our
everyday conversation. Mary and Martha embody the struggle
between "being" and "doing." Parables of the seed and sower
and of the good Samaritan give us instant images that help
us understand complex issues of personal growth and social
justice.

Drawing on rich biblical and theological language gives us
tools for engaging in theological reflection and helps us build
spiritual muscles. Increasing muscle strength, especially muscle
that has not been used for a while, takes time and practice, and
perhaps patience. In new-member classes at my church, I hear
time and again from people who attended church school as a
child and left the church as adolescents. Through such life experiences as marriage, childbirth, or some crisis, adults return
to church. I hear people comment that they just have a "Sunday school" faith. On the one hand, having the faith of a child
is awesome and wonderful, with a ready assurance of God's
presence. On the other hand, whatever our age or background,
our faith needs to mature. We need to find language to express
our faith, our belief in God, and the ways God is at work in our
lives.

At 13 years old, Lilly had become aware of the number of
people she saw begging on the streets of her town. She became
indignant that God would "let this happen." Her childlike assurance that God was in control of everything was challenged
by the chilling reality of poverty and need. Upset and con-
fused, she talked to me after church one day. "I do not believe
in God any more. If God really existed, God would help poor,
homeless people," she declared. I think she expected me to be
just as devastated and shocked as she was, with her previously
solid faith crumbling around her. On the contrary, I saw this
declaration as a wonderful opportunity for theological reflection. I asked her to tell me more about what she was feeling

and how she thought God worked. As she talked, she began to grapple with how God is at work through our actions. She realized that we could be the hands of God by reaching out to people in need and that God existed through our actions. Yet she also thought about social sin that allowed people to go hungry. We talked about some of the reasons why people might find themselves in such situations, and she began to think about what it meant when we talked in church of "seeing the face of Jesus in others." Lilly's faith had been deeply shaken; yet through theological reflection, she found language to express her faith. She also found a renewed and maturing faith.

Theological Reflection as Lifelong Journey

Theological reflection is part of a lifelong faith journey, one that requires being open to whatever may arise along the road. As my son negotiates his way from teenage years into adulthood, he is discovering that adults, particularly his parents, do not have clear answers to all of life's problems. He is becoming aware that he needs to be open to what lies ahead, whether joyful or painful. Spiritual maturity comes from working through issues as they arise, not from figuring them out ahead of time—as if that were possible.

Maturing is painful. In our spiritual tradition, the phrase "dark night of the soul" describes the agony that grips us from time to time as we struggle with our faith. Ultimately, that struggle brings a renewed faith and a deeper assurance of God's love and presence. As we wrestle with such complex issues as why bad things happen to good people, we realize that no easy answers emerge. My students, eager to solve all the pastoral problems in their field-education placements, realize that learning to live with ambiguity makes more sense than looking for answers. A mature faith embraces complexity.

Sometimes complexity and ambiguity become so burdensome that faith is crushed. A crisis of faith may be so traumatic that people turn away from the church and from God. A woman whose young daughter died after a dreadful battle with cancer was grief-stricken and angry with God. Over and over she said, "Why would God let this happen?" As she met with me for pastoral care, I talked about a God who does not let children die, about a God who walks beside her in her grief, a God who weeps tears of sorrow along with her. At times like this, the faith community carries us, offering prayers when we are unable to pray, believing in God when belief seems barren or impossible. When I had a miscarriage after trying for several years to become pregnant, I was angry with God and railed against a God who I thought had expelled this new life within me so easily. I was ready to abandon God. Fortunately, God did not abandon me. Through a process of grieving, reflecting on psalms that allowed me to lament, and receiving pastoral care from my faith community, friends and family, I found courage to continue the journey of life and faith.

The journey of faith is complex and sometimes painful. It takes courage to embark on this journey, to stay the course when faced with personal and theological challenges. Theological reflection is a tool that helps us along the way to gain the wisdom that comes from contemplation upon experience and learning from mistakes. Whether we are considering personal or spiritual maturity, we need to be open to the journey and ready to reflect on God's spirit at work. Rather than having answers, we need to be ready to answer God's call.

What Makes Our Reflection Theological?

I was standing at the sink with my hands in hot, soapy water, doing the supper dishes—a daily chore that I disliked. It was boring and repetitive. So I decided to reflect theologically on washing the dishes. The situation was simple. Every night I washed the dishes that had accumulated over the day. It was a necessary chore, and while I did not enjoy the task, I did enjoy having a clean and tidy kitchen. My mind wandered as I imagined all the dishes I have washed over my life stacked end to end, circling the earth, and all the dishes I have yet to do in what I hope are many years to come. So what does this repetitive task have to do with God?

I thought about my choice to use an environmentally friendly dishwashing liquid, my small contribution to caring for the earth. More than that, dishwashing is quiet, uninterrupted time, since family members seem to disappear at this particular moment. Also, this task does not require me to think, so for the first time in my day my mind is free to wander, an activity I find relaxing. As my mind wanders, I sort through the day's frustrations, remember tasks I need to do, think about family members. Suddenly, it occurred to me that this was a sacred time, similar to prayer or meditation. As I thought about where God's spirit was at work, I began to see my day in a different way. Reviewing what had happened, I gave thanks to God for moments of satisfaction. I let go of frustrations. I tried to see others as God might see them, as beloved children of God—an easier exercise when thinking of some people than others!

I prayed for family members who were struggling with illness or tired from caring for those who were ill. Deep into my meditative mindset, I realized that I had run out of dishes and felt sad that this time had come to a close. Reflecting theologically on this mundane task had been satisfying and refreshing and gave me a totally new approach to doing the dishes. I have never looked at washing dishes in the same way since. It has become a holy, contemplative time.

As we think about doing theological reflection, trying to be more intentional about reflecting theologically, a question arises: What makes it theological? Do we need to use big theological words like "justification" and "sanctification"? Should we choose situations that present clear spiritual issues? Can we engage in theological reflection if we do not know much about the Bible? How "religious" do we need to be?

Basically, we are *theologically* reflecting when we ask "Where is God is in this?" or "What does God want me to learn from this?" We do not need to use explicitly theological language, and while the recall of some biblical stories is enriching, we do not need to be biblical scholars. Prayer and attendance at worship will enrich our faith but are not essential to doing theological reflection. And we do not need to be particularly religious or pious. In thinking about where God is present, we can ponder all aspects of our life—everything from ordinary routines like doing the dishes to the largest existential questions.

God is present in all aspects of our lives, both the large existential experiences of birth and death as well as in routine, ordinary happenings. In a sense the ordinary *is* extraordinary. That we live, breathe, walk and talk, think and laugh, deduce and create, and daily find the courage to continue living what seem to be ordinary lives—all this is totally extraordinary. Theological reflection can encompass our whole life. I believe theological reflection is finding God in the extraordinary nature of ordinary day-to-day living.

How Do We Reflect Theologically?

Beyond asking ourselves, "Where is God in this situation?" we can add other questions to deepen our reflection such as:

1. Where is God for others?
2. What biblical stories or images come to mind?
3. What theological themes or concepts come to mind?
4. What church traditions connect with this event?

"Where is God in this situation?" is a simple question inviting us to name the movement of God's spirit in a particular event. The other questions encourage us to deepen our reflection. For instance, the partner question, "Where is God for others?" challenges us to think about differences in theological perspective. While we need to be aware of how we understand God and God's activity in the world, we need to take into account the views of others. We could ask where God might be for each of the people in a situation and discover that each person has a different perspective.

In one congregation where I served, the organ started to make odd noises during worship. Repairs to delicate reeds were needed. Getting this small repair done raised a question about the general state of the pipe organ. Band-Aid repairs were not going to suffice any longer. It looked as though a complete overhaul was needed, and that would be expensive. I know many congregations that have faced similar situations. Some congregation members wanted to raise money to make substantial repairs that would enhance the organ's sound, encourage congregational hymn-singing, and enable the organist to better support worship that would express God's glory. Other members had a different perspective. They preferred to spend money to assist people in need, rather than putting it into bricks and mortar. In reflecting theologically, we became aware of a diversity of perspectives that all had God's spirit at work. So, rather than simply assuming that God was present in one viewpoint over another, we concluded that God could be present in both. So we did both things—raised money to rejuvenate the church organ and began raising funds to sponsor a refugee family.

Being attentive to our own sense of where God is present, as well as to other perspectives, gives us a more complex yet more mature faith.

What Biblical Stories or Images Come to Mind?

Making biblical connections in our theological reflection can be challenging. Most people have a skimpy biblical background and use up their repertoire of stories fairly quickly. Also it is difficult to make connections between a situation and a Scripture passage unless the text relates explicitly to the experience. In addition, we tend to choose Bible stories that support our positions rather than passages that challenge us.

A group leader, or other members of the group, can offer biblical stories that come to mind if people are unable to make their own connections. These stories can have a clear link to the event or can challenge our perspective. Mary had been part of her congregation from birth. She had a deep faith that was inspiring, yet at times she moved too quickly toward the positive. She often declared that God does not give us more than we can handle. Group members reminded her that Jesus, bowed down by pain and despair, cried out, "My God, my God, why have you abandoned me?" Sometimes we need to acknowledge our pain. Sometimes we need to cry out in our sense of abandonment. As Mary thought about this further, she explored the Psalms, writings that express fear, anger, agony, or shame. She began to realize that God is able to listen to the full range of our feelings and to respond in love.

When challenged by biblical stories, we may find ourselves surprised by what we learn. When Dave worked in the "Out-of-the-Cold" program, an outreach mission to street people, he heard Jesus' call to care for the "little ones" as a challenge to his life of relative wealth. Dave knew he lived a privileged life. Bible texts calling us to feed and clothe the poor really tugged at his heart. Instead of just feeling guilty, Dave wanted to do something. He wanted to give not only money but also his time to help those less fortunate. What surprised him were the relationships he formed. People at the mission were no longer the "little ones" or those "less fortunate." They were Joe and Sadie and Ben, real people with real life stories. Dave found himself looking forward to his times at the mission, catching up on people's lives. He also discovered that Joe and Sadie and Ben were interested in his life. He was making friends.

The biblical text comes alive when reflected in our daily living. Making connections between our stories and the biblical stories both supports and challenges our ways of seeing God at work.

What Theological Themes or Concepts Come to Mind?

As I mentioned earlier, most people are not comfortable calling themselves "theologians" and consequently lack confidence in gaining access to theological themes or concepts. Some imagine that being a theologian is about knowing long words and theological concepts, and that theologians are far removed from our daily lives. Yet theological language is deeply embedded within us without our realizing it. Theological concepts are embedded in the following words: church, worship, prayer, confession, assurance, praise, sermon, preaching, hymnody, offering, intercession, thanksgiving, Word of God, Gospel, Scripture, commissioning, blessing, and benediction. These words are familiar to us from our weekly worship.

We think about other theological concepts through our work on church committees. Our Christian education committees are concerned with passing on our faith and nurturing faith development. Our stewardship committees attempt to be good stewards of our resources, being accountable to one another and to God. Other committees draw us to reflect on other theological aspects of being faithful Christians— such as worship, ministry and personnel, pastoral care, and outreach.

When we worship, listen to sermons, and participate in Bible study groups, we hear about God, Jesus, the Holy Spirit, the Trinity, evil, sin, forgiveness, redemption, reconciliation, suffering, justice, love, hope, joy, salvation, revelation, grace, holiness, faith, baptism, communion, sacraments, community, and so on.

Our church year teaches us another layer of theological language: Advent, waiting, Christmas, birth, Epiphany, Ash Wednesday, Lent, journey, Holy Week, Good Friday, crucifixion, Easter, resurrection, Pentecost, tongues of fire, birth of the church, spiritual gifts.

In our prayers we hear and speak images for God that shape our faith, images such as creator, father, mother, holy one, brooding hen, almighty, and justice seeker. Our words for Jesus Christ further stretch our understanding of God: Messiah, suffering servant, Son of God, Lord, God-made-flesh, shepherd, brother, lover. We are steeped in theological language and theological concepts, often without being aware of how much we know. Through theological reflection, we can gain access to this knowledge to sharpen our theological thinking.

What Church Traditions Connect with This Event?

Through the generations, people have grappled with what it means to live faithfully. Each generation draws on what has gone before; at the same time, it seeks to discern what needs to change in our present world. In some matters, consensus is found. For instance, after great debate, an international ecumenical agreement about baptism was reached. In other matters, practices differ among denominations, as in the ordination of women. As we reflect theologically, we can learn of ancient and recent history within our church, to add to the wisdom from those who have gone before. That history will contribute to our ongoing discernment.

Recently, in my own denomination, the United Church of Canada, we have been called to account for our treatment of Native peoples. We believed we were being faithful years ago by taking Native children away from their parents to attend residential schools. Children were separated from their parents for years at a time, forbidden to speak their own language, and abused physically and sexually. As we listen to the pain of our Native brothers and sisters today, we are called to repent of previous actions, and we are moved to find paths to reconciliation. While it is an agonizing journey, we believe that God's justice and reconciliation are at work. Theological reflection draws us to live faithfully as we critically examine previous actions and learn anew God's call on our lives.

Continuing the Story

Theological reflection is a process of discerning where and how God is present and at work in our lives, against a backdrop of the biblical story, theological themes and concepts, and our church traditions. Through this process we join a great cloud of witnesses, those who followed Jesus and tried to discern what it meant to live a life committed to Christ. As we reflect, we can hear echoes of voices from the past offering wisdom for our reflection. Drawing on Scripture and church tradition keeps us grounded in the faith of those pilgrims who have gone before us, giving us a sense of whence we have come, and freeing us to move into an unknown future. We may deal with situations and events that challenged previous theological traditions. We can take courage from those ancestors who tried to address the pastoral concerns of their day, just as we are called to reflect on our experiences, shedding light on how to live the gospel message in our time and place. In this way, we join the continually unfolding story.

3

Life of the Group

HAVING LOOKED AT THEOLOGICAL REFLECTION in a general way in the last two chapters, let's begin to look at how to do it both as a personal spiritual discipline and in a group setting. Whether it's a personal journey or a group process, logistics must be considered, such as advertising, scheduling, organizing, mentoring, and facilitating. One of the most important items in this list is the role of facilitator, or group leader. In a group setting, a facilitator is the one who invites participants into the process of reflection, encourages the group to be comfortable sharing with one another, and monitors the ongoing life of the group. Let us begin to look at the facilitator's role in more detail.

Role of the Facilitator

I believe that the success of any small group is in its leadership. A skilled leader can help participants feel comfortable as they get to know one another and share thoughts and feelings. The group does not need to be managed but gently coached. It does not need to be controlled but rather led in an open and consultative fashion.

If you are an experienced facilitator, you may want to think about your leadership style. What gifts do you bring to this work? What growing edges do you want to work on? Even after years of leading various groups, I always learn something new in my role as facilitator. What I learn changes over time. After learning the basics of group life, such as leaving space for silence and listening more carefully, I moved on to other growing edges, such as being aware of different learning styles in group members and how that affects group life. Constantly learning keeps me aware of my role and keeps my outlook fresh as I anticipate a new group and feel excitement about what discoveries lie ahead. Being open to what I might learn prevents me from becoming stale and keeps me attentive to the unique aspects of each group. While I set myself a goal for improving my skills as facilitator, I have found that some learning is serendipitous, such as an occasion when a group member offers unexpected feedback. Nonetheless, set a definite goal, such as finding gentle ways to encourage discussion, or working on being more assertive in offering new directions for group discussion. A goal can be skill-oriented or it can have a broader focus. For example, a learning goal could be an effort to increase awareness of God's spirit of grace in the group discussion by naming moments of inspiration and revelation. Be creative as you look forward to a new group.

If you are new to this specialized form of group leadership, you will quickly discover that there are many tasks to consider and aspects of the group to organize. What follows in this chapter is a hands-on outline for how to put together a theological reflection group—from advertisement to scheduling to the small-group meeting itself. However, if facilitating a group is new for you, you may feel nervous. You may wonder whether you can carry it off with confidence. I hope the suggestions in this chapter will equip you with what you need to be a facilitator. While you can do much to prepare yourself, the best learning will come through experience. As you lead a group, you will find out what works and what does not work, and you will discover your own distinct style of leadership. If you view this venture as an ongoing learning experience, you can relax a little.

You may worry whether anyone will show up. In part, you need to trust that if this is the right time for such a group, then people will sign up for it. You have no control over whether the idea will spark people's imagination. Yet my experience is that people are hungry for this kind of discussion in congregational life. They are thirsty for a greater awareness of God's presence in their lives. If they do not find a theological reflection group engaging now, try offering it at another time. It's amazing that something that did not seem to catch people's attention one year is the "flavor of the month" the next year.

While you can do many things to prepare yourself to facilitate a group, questions always crop up—such as whether people will blend well together or whether they will enjoy their experience in the group. Rather than worrying about such questions, I take a step back and look at my own area of responsibility and the responsibility that belongs to the group as a whole. As facilitator, I am responsible for initiating the group and encouraging discussion. Within the group, all participants are responsible for the way they cooperate as respectful listeners and mutual learners. We all share responsibility for the successful life of the group. More will be said about how to share this responsibility in a section on group covenant.

As you deal with the logistics of setting up a theological reflection group, remember that the purpose of this experience is to learn about God's presence in our lives. We are learning about living our baptismal covenant to serve God. We are learning how to be a small community of faith; and as facilitators, we are learning what it means to offer our gifts of leadership to God's people with confidence and humility. Learning is exciting because it opens up new possibilities, yet it can be scary because it invites us into the unknown. As adults, we much prefer to have all the answers, or at least appear to have the answers. Also, some of us may not have set aside time to think about our faith in years, and some may be new to a faith life. As learners we may struggle to put into words what we believe, and consequently we may be nervous about appearing foolish. An effective facilitator encourages the creation of a safe place to learn, invites people to speak about their faith, and prompts them to find the words to say what is in their hearts. The role of facilitator is an important and exciting one, so take a deep breath and get engaged.

In preparing to facilitate, here are three suggestions that will be beneficial whether you are new to this task or experienced. First, before each meeting, I pray for our time together, asking for God's wisdom in our deliberations, praying for each individual, focusing on an image of this person's face and the issues in his or her life. This prayer reminds me that my role is not simply to accomplish a task but to become aware of the fragility of people's lives and their need for the sustaining, nurturing presence of God. Prayer reminds me that God is part of this group experience as well as part of all other aspects of our lives. As we enter this process of theological reflection, we are trying to become more aware of God's active presence in our lives. We are trying to see God more clearly. For this to happen, we need to be aware that God is looking just as actively for a relationship with us as we are with God.

Second, if you have not done theological reflection before, try it out a few times yourself. I do not like to invite people to join me in a process that I have not experienced myself. Use the model offered in chapter 4, and write several reflections in the weeks leading up to the first meeting. You will discover where the sticking points occur for you, where you find challenge in reflecting, and where you find affirmation.

Finally, keep a journal of the experience as it unfolds, right from the beginning. As you start to think about leading the group, write down your hopes and fears, what you want to accomplish, and what makes you feel nervous. Ask God for what you need to get the group underway and for openness to address whatever may arise. As the group life unfolds, keeping this journal gives you an opportunity to reflect on what has taken place in each meeting, noting the "Aha!" moments when people learned something new, and noting also those times when you felt awkward in your role and would like to try something different. Ultimately, journal writing encourages you to reflect theologically on your leadership role and maintains coherence with the whole process. You are not asking people to do something that you are not willing to do yourself.

Offering an Invitation

Theological reflection can unfold in a variety of ways. You may choose to use the theological reflection process as a personal spiritual journey and not be part of any group. Or you may choose to organize the theological reflection process as a group experience. Groups can vary. A group may be composed of congregation members, friends, or colleagues. For instance, a group of chaplains from different hospitals decided that they would do theological reflection together for spiritual renewal and collegial support.

If this is a personal journey, without a group component, then set aside time each day or once a week for theological reflection. Be faithful about the time you set aside, noting it in your calendar, making an appointment with yourself for reflection time with God. I find that if I do not make that appointment with myself, other activities fill my day and I lose the opportunity for this important conversation with God. Also, to enrich this experience, consider finding a mentor or partner, someone with whom to be in conversation, whether in person or by e-mail. Invite someone you can trust with your deepest thoughts and feelings. A conversation partner blesses us with a different perspective. Sometimes we cannot see the woods for the trees, so another viewpoint offers encouragement and challenge in our spiritual journey.

However, if this theological reflection experience is being offered in a group setting, decide how to invite people to be part of the group. If you are inviting friends or colleagues, then it will be a personal invitation. If inviting congregation members, you can ask particular people who you feel will benefit from this group experience, or you can issue a general invitation. You can announce this opportunity through your worship bulletin or church newsletter. You can make announcements during worship or at other gatherings, offer a brief skit, or have it mentioned in a sermon. Two sample bulletin announcements are offered on page 45 that you can use or adapt. You know your context best and can decide what will work to catch people's attention and interest.

Group Make-Up

Ideally, a group of six to eight people works well, creating meetings with enough members to encourage a healthy discussion, along with some diversity of thought and opinion. If a group has more than eight, quieter members may not have a chance to get involved in conversation. Having fewer than five in a group can be a problem, too. If one person is absent, then the group will feel too small for fruitful conversation. However, you are the expert in your own context and will know what number of people works best for groups at your church. I know groups of 10 people that have worked well, especially when they are attentive to ensuring space for everyone to speak. I also know a group of three who were committed to faithful attendance and experienced great benefit from the stimulating and intimate conversation. A final factor in considering the size of the group is the number of meetings; more about this will be explained later.

Bulletin Announcement 1

REFLECTING WITH GOD IN COMMUNITY

As Christians, we believe that God exists as a loving presence in our lives. So how do we connect with that loving presence in our daily activities? How do we take our Sunday morning faith into our home life, our workplace, and our community?

To address these questions, a small group of six to eight people will gather weekly [biweekly, monthly] to reflect on issues arising in their lives and to explore how God is present. If you are interested, but you are not sure what is involved, or whether you could be involved in such a group, please speak to [facilitator's name and contact information].

[*For later bulletins:*Three people have expressed interest to this point, so please consider being one of the next five.]

[Add starting date and meeting times and place.]

Let us gather to reflect on God's presence in our daily lives.

Bulletin Announcement 2

WHAT'S GOD GOT TO DO WITH IT?

What does God have to do with our lives? Is there any connection between Sunday morning and the rest of the week? How does my faith have an impact on my life? If you are asking these kind of questions, then [name of group] might be just what you're looking for. [Name of group] is a gathering of six to eight people who will meet [how often] to talk about what God has to do with our daily lives.

Interested? Have questions? Contact [facilitator's name] at [contact information].

Finally, here's your chance to ask the really hard question: What does God have to do with my daily life?

Another aspect of group make-up to consider is diversity or homogeneity. You may want to think about incorporating a balance of male and female; a range of ages; a variety of church, workplace, and life experience; gay and straight; and people from several ethnic groups. Diversity offers a variety of viewpoints, life experiences, and faith perspectives. Or you may prefer to have a more homogeneous group that will focus on common issues. For instance, one women's group that gathered regularly in my church decided to engage in theological reflection. Or members of a congregational group, such as the Christian education committee, may want to focus on theological reflection to deepen their understanding of their Christian call through baptism and to clarify a vision for their work. Or a youth group may want to reflect on decisions they need to make at this point in their lives.

I have placed announcements in the church bulletin many times, inviting people to be part of a theological reflection group. Sometimes, a few people have responded, thus creating one small group of six. At other times, I have had so many people indicate interest that I have formed two or three groups. So what do I do when 20 people respond to the invitation? I create three groups if I have the time, or offer one group now and arrange a waiting list for everyone else. When I schedule multiple groups, they often divide up neatly, determined by agreed-upon meeting times. Some people prefer to meet during the day. Others have only evening times available. I had one set of people who liked to preserve weekday evenings for family activities; consequently, they wanted to meet with me on a Sunday night. As facilitator, you need to determine your limits of time and energy and your flexibility in scheduling. Or a number of people in your congregation may have the skills for and interest in leading a reflection group, so a number of facilitators could lead groups.

If you are a new facilitator, I suggest that you try leading only one group rather than several groups. This choice will give you a clearer focus and be less stressful as your first experience. Whoever the group members are, however the group was formed, each person is unique and beloved by God, and the group has God's spirit firmly embedded in its midst.

Setting a Schedule

At times, setting a schedule can be a challenge. People's lives are busy, going in many directions. One method of setting meeting times is to set out a course of meetings that suit your own timetable and then to invite those who are able to join you, naming times and dates in your announcements and invitations. Another method is to gather everyone together for an initial meeting to get to know one another and introduce the process. At that meeting, a schedule for subsequent meetings can be established by the whole group.

If more people respond to your invitation than can fit in one group, have a brief meeting after worship with everyone interested to decide how to divide up into several groups and when these groups can meet. You may find that the meeting schedule will dictate who goes in which group. Some groups are happy to meet weekly. Others prefer every two to three weeks. One group met irregularly, setting its schedule to accommodate the busy lives and travel schedules of retired and working people. While I am flexible about meeting times, I have found that having meetings more than one month apart can be problematic. With too much time between meetings, the momentum and focus are easily lost. Of course, with this point in mind, take into account busy times in the year such as Christmas and less busy seasons when people are away, such as summer months. Whatever the meeting schedules, I prefer to be flexible and work around the timetables of group members rather than set too many rules.

Generally, I prefer that meetings be only two hours long. Respecting the busyness of people's lives and the multitude of responsibilities they are juggling is important. Also, I believe people's concentration on one focus or point of interest wanes after two hours. Listening well is hard work! Conversely, having less than two hours will make participants feel rushed. Initially, people wonder how they will fill the time and if they will have anything worthwhile to say. Later, as they gain experience and confidence, they find that time flies by and they want more time for discussion.

A theological reflection group may choose to gather over a long period of time, yet I suggest that one of the positive aspects of this group is its short-term commitment. In a busy congregation or with people whose busy lives prevent them from committing themselves for an extended period, a short-term commitment is more suitable. People who wish to continue with the process can join up with another group offered at another time. In this way, people in the congregation will get to know each other well in different group configurations.

Meeting Location

The location for meetings is important. It needs to be a quiet, private space where people feel comfortable talking about their lives and their faith. Initially, people may feel tentative in talking about God, so having a sense of privacy and quiet is necessary. One group met in the privacy of my church office. However, because we met on a busy Tuesday night, we could hear the scouts playing their games, various meetings taking place, and ballet-class music filtering down from the second floor. We moved to the sanctuary, in another part of the building, and found there a quiet and sacred space. My office worked well at other times in the week when there was less noise or activity.

Meeting in people's homes is possible, so long as there are no interruptions by family members, phones, dogs, callers at the door, and other normal aspects of life that intervene. A neutral, quiet space is ideal for optimizing comfort for all as they open their hearts to one another and to God.

Outline of Meetings

Meetings can be structured in various ways. What works best is to have two introductory meetings, then enough subsequent meetings to allow everyone an opportunity to offer a theological-reflection presentation, followed by one last meeting for wrap-up, evaluation, and celebration. Thus, if you have a group of six, you will have a total of nine meetings. If you have a group of eight, you will have a total of 11 meetings.

The following outline of meetings is a suggestion. You may find that one introductory meeting will suffice, especially if people know one another already. If a group has been through this process before, participants will prefer to plunge straight into theological reflection and will not need the introductory meetings. Also, some groups complete the final evaluation and celebration as part of the last theological-reflection meeting, making the final meeting slightly longer.

SESSION 1: INTRODUCTION
- Welcome people and do icebreaker exercise or opening.
- Develop a group covenant.
- Describe the process.
- Set dates and times of all sessions.
- Set schedule of theological reflection presentations.
- Hand out "Reflecting with God" (outline, p. 62).
- End with wrap-up.
- Close with prayer, meditation, or poem.

SESSION 2: INTRODUCTION
- Open with prayer, meditation, or poem.
- "Check in" with one another.
- Revisit and establish group covenant.
- Get to know one another: pattern of a typical day.
- End with wrap-up.
- Close with prayer, meditation, or poem.

SUBSEQUENT SESSIONS:
THEOLOGICAL REFLECTION PRESENTATIONS

Each person in the group is assigned a meeting at
which he or she will present a theological reflection,
followed by group discussion.

GROUP PROCESS	APPROXIMATE TIMES
• Opening prayer, meditation, or poem	10 minutes
• Check-in	15 minutes
• Presentation of theological reflection	15 minutes
• Break	10 minutes
• Group discussion	50 minutes
• Wrap-up	10 minutes
• Closing prayer, meditation, or poem	10 minutes

LAST SESSION: SAYING GOODBYE

- Evaluation of time together
- Refreshments or meal
- Closing rituals

Elements of Sessions

Introductory sessions offer a time to get to know one another,
establishing group norms of trust and mutual respect. What
follows is a description of the various components of these sessions as suggestions for developing your group's life.

Icebreaker and Opening

Before plunging into the waters of sharing our lives and our
faith, we need to get to the edge of the lake. Some people are
brave enough to plunge into cold water and find it exhilarat-
ing. But most people prefer to wade gently into warm water
with assurances of their safety. Thus the two introductory meetings invite people to dip a toe into warm water and encourage
them to enter more deeply.

In the very first session, have an icebreaking activity to get people talking with one another quickly, and to alleviate any nervousness. One icebreaker that works well is to ask people to give their name and to share briefly one highlight from their day with one other person in the group. After a few minutes' discussion, ask people to introduce the person with whom they were speaking. In this way, the group begins by encouraging people to listen to one another. Other icebreakers might include talking about your involvement in the congregation, or sharing a significant childhood experience of church, or talking about an object or symbol that is personally meaningful and explaining why.

In every session, begin with an opening such as a prayer, a reading from Scripture, a meditation, or a poem—something to set the focus for the session. As the group gathers, coming from different contexts and experiences, it helps to focus the time together with a brief opening. You may be comfortable praying spontaneously, or perhaps offering a prepared written prayer such as the one below. Sometimes the reading or poem might be connected to the theme of the theological-reflection presentation, but it need not necessarily be connected. What has been uncanny, perhaps even serendipitous, in my experience, is that when the reading or poem has not been intentionally connected to the presentation theme, it often has an unforeseen connection.

OPENING PRAYER

Gracious God, we give thanks for the opportunity to meet together for reflection and growth. We know you are with us in every moment, yet in our busy lives we forget that you are as close as our breathing. Sharpen our awareness of your presence in our discussion, so we may see you more clearly in our lives. Sustain our faith so we may feel you more nearly. Amen.

Establishing a Group Covenant

For people to feel safe and comfortable sharing significant issues, establish a group covenant of shared behaviors and values. Whether this is a congregational group in which everyone assumes shared beliefs, a group of close friends who assume they know one another well, or a group of work colleagues with shared values, making these assumptions explicit puts everyone on the same page.

I prefer to develop the covenant as a group, rather than to set these norms for the group as facilitator. I begin by asking people to think for a moment about various groups in which they have participated. Have them think about what was helpful in those groups and what was unhelpful. Then invite people to say what is important for them in this group experience. At this first meeting, I simply collect everyone's thoughts on newsprint in whatever ways they are offered, without discussion. At our second introductory meeting, when people have an opportunity to go back to this group covenant, they can add to what was offered or clarify anything they did not understand. This amended covenant can be written more clearly on newsprint for all future sessions. Displaying the covenant at every meeting, as a backdrop for group life and discussion etiquette, ensures that each person feels safe and comfortable in sharing his or her life with others. One idea for a group covenant is found on page 54.

Ultimately, a group covenant is an explicit statement of how you would like the group to unfold, offering shared behaviors such as starting and ending on time and shared values such as respecting one another. Developing this covenant takes seriously the needs of individuals as they participate with mutuality and respect. It also takes seriously the biblical stories of God's desire for relationship. God made a covenant with Noah to care for and protect all creation. God made a covenant with Abram and Sarai that they would be ancestors of many nations. In the book of Jeremiah, God made a covenant with the Israelites saying, "I will put my law within them, and I will write it on their hearts; and I will be their God and they shall be my people." As God's people we are accountable to one another, loving our neighbor as ourselves in all our sessions.

Describe the Process

As you begin, give the group an overview of all the sessions as well as a description of the theological reflection process as outlined on page 62 of chapter 4. Give group members a copy of the outline to follow as you explain the process (see appendix). If you are familiar with the process, then you can use your own words to describe it. If you are new to the process, then you may want to use sections of this book to convey what is involved.

In addition, you may want to describe the format of each session, so that people can see the shape of the meetings. Typically, I have that format clearly displayed at each meeting so that people will know what is coming up and in what order. An outline for the group process, such as the one offered above, visibly displayed in the meeting room, gives everyone a sense of what happens next. While groups can feel free to vary from the outline, particularly with experienced group leaders, the suggestions are designed to assist those who have never tried small-group work before.

Schedules and Presentations

It will be important to schedule all meeting dates, if that has not already been done. Also, decide who will offer a theological reflection presentation on which meeting date. Typically, a moment of silence will greet your question about who is willing to go first. But usually one brave person will start the ball rolling. If no one is immediately willing, you may decide to come back to the task of scheduling in session 2. As a new

---

SAMPLE GROUP COVENANT

From a common ground of Christian community at All Saints Church and from a commitment to the purpose of our "Reflecting with God" group, we will:

- Have respect and consideration for ourselves and others.
- Share with each other when we are ready.
- Attend sessions to the best of our ability.
- Understand that sessions will start and end on time.
- Allow and respect differences between people.
- Hold what is shared in the group as confidential.

---

facilitator, relax, because the schedule will fall into place one way or another.

Hand out "Reflecting with God" at the first session so that people who are offering their theological reflection in earlier sessions can begin to look at the questions.

Wrap-up

Each session will end with an opportunity to reflect on what has been helpful during the time together and then conclude with a brief closing prayer, meditation, or poem.

Once the time allotted for discussion comes to an end, or perhaps when the discussion has wound down to a natural conclusion, then the facilitator asks for a moment of silence for the group to reflect on what has been important about the time together. It is not a time for getting back into the issue. It is a time to think about the meeting as a whole. A facilitator might ask, "What has been helpful or unhelpful in our time together today?" This question encourages people to be aware of the group's life. Often people will say that the discussion was exciting or moving, or that the presentation was thoughtful and clear.

Sometimes people may have other group-life issues on their mind. For instance, if one person is dominating group discussion, another member may at this time gently suggest that enough space should be provided for everyone to be heard. It can be hard to name group dynamics that are unhelpful, so a facilitator may want to bring up this topic at an early occasion. A simple example, such as "It was unhelpful to have so much noise from the group next door as we got into our discussion" illustrates how to name something that is not helpful to the group. This intervention gives people permission to name issues that will enhance group life. Also, referring to the group covenant can remind people of agreed-upon behaviors and values. For instance, if someone felt that an idea they suggested was not treated respectfully by the group, that person could refer to the group covenant as a reminder of what everyone agreed to at the outset.

Closing: Prayer, Meditation, Poem

Offering a closing prayer, meditation, or poem focuses the group for concluding its time together and heading back into diverse lives. The closing can be a simple blessing: "We have been blessed by this time together to get to know one another more deeply. May God continue to bless us in the days ahead until we meet again. Amen." Or, a group member could offer a brief, spontaneous prayer lifting up the concerns and thanksgivings expressed in the group discussion. Otherwise, a brief poem or Scripture reading offers a way to bring the time to a close and to send people back into their lives.

Check-In

After the first session, I suggest that you include a time for "checking in" with one another in all subsequent sessions. The purpose of checking in is to say what is necessary to be fully present in the group. Rather than a recital of everything that happened this week, from taking the dog to the vet to deciding what to cook for dinner, check-in is a brief focused time to catch up with the group on events as they pertain to group life. If there is a great deal going on for people, it is a time to name those things, put them to one side, and begin to focus on the session. Checking in with one another plays an important function in building group life and maintaining connections from meeting to meeting. In addition, people may want to update the group on what has developed in their lives as a result of the group life in general or a theological reflection presentation in particular.

In facilitating this segment of the meeting, watch the time. Take care to allot enough time for all elements of the session, as suggested in the outline above. As you develop your group covenant, you may want to decide on the amount of time for person to check in. Occasionally, more time needs to be taken during check-in because of a particular issue that has arisen; however, that time needs to be agreed upon by the group as a whole.

The Pattern of a Typical Day

An exercise useful in a second introductory session is sharing something of our lives with one another. We need to get to know one another better so we can listen carefully to the issues brought for discussion by individuals in subsequent sessions. One way to do this is to have people describe a typical day. Often, in congregational life, we have little knowledge of the day-to-day routines that others follow or the work they do. By hearing about the lives others live, we begin to see threads that are common to us all, as well as the particular strands that make each life unique. Sometimes people will say that no day is typical, because their schedules are so varied. Nonetheless, hearing some of what goes into daily life gives us a sense of what people confront each day.

A detailed description of subsequent sessions is offered in chapter 5.

Group Life

In initial sessions, members may express strong opinions about the covenant or the meeting space or personal needs. If you are a new facilitator, these statements may be a little unnerving. However, strongly expressed viewpoints are a way of establishing personal space and testing the flexibility of leadership. As facilitator, respond to these views by inviting people to take some initiative in decision making. If they are unsure about the covenant, ask them what they would like to change. If they are unhappy with the meeting space, ask them for suggestions about a new space. Inviting this initiative contributes to group formation, with each gifted person valued for his or her presence in the group. I find that when people have a hand in organizing the schedule for sessions and in developing the group covenant, they become more comfortable with proceeding. Take people's needs seriously, yet do not get so bogged down that you cannot proceed. When in doubt, ask the group members what they think about an expressed view or suggestion offered, and have everyone take responsibility for how to proceed. Or you can always agree to think about an issue that emerges and return to it at the next session if no consensus is reached. When an issue is revisited in a subsequent session, time has gone by, allowing feelings to settle and insights to emerge.

If you have read about or taken a Myers-Briggs Type Indicator workshop, you will know about the many different personality types. If you have not, you know from life experience that people are unique in their styles of behaving and being with others. Rather than expecting everyone to conform to my sense of how they should behave in a group, I assume that everyone is different and will offer a unique perspective to group life. For instance, some people are very quiet and need time to think before they speak. Others will offer their thoughts even before they know what they think. I do not assume that quieter people should speak more or that more vocal people should talk less. Each person makes a different contribution to the group. However, I do try to give space for quieter people to offer thoughts, and I do monitor the amount of speaking done by a more talkative person. It is the task of the facilitator to monitor and balance the needs of each individual in relation to the whole group. If in doubt, use the wrap-up time at the end of each session to check with people about the group life and how it is working.

Having looked at some of the organizational aspects of this group, let's get to the heart of the matter—theological reflection with God in community.

4

Heart of the Matter

LET US GET TO THE HEART OF THE MATTER by looking at how to do theological reflection. This chapter offers an outline titled "Reflecting with God" (pages 62-63), and a description of how this process works. "Reflecting with God" is a series of questions to encourage reflection that can be used as a personal journey or in small-group gatherings. Basically, this process is designed to encourage conversation with God through reflection on daily life.

If you choose to do this reflection as a personal spiritual journey, you can use the reflective questions to think about an event or situation. The questions encourage you to examine feelings and thoughts; they also invite you to make biblical and faith connections. If you are offering this process in small-group sessions, the reflective questions can be used by each group member and presented to the group for discussion. The small group may be made up of members of a congregation, a gathering of friends, or a group of colleagues. For instance, a woman working as a parish nurse decided that her parish nurse colleagues could enhance their pastoral practice by means of theological reflection. She gathered a group of parish nurses working in various congregations and invited them to deepen the connection between nursing practice and congregational ministry through theological reflection. Small-group gatherings enrich personal reflection with God, with the addition of further insights through discussion with others. The underlying assumption is that through a faith community, God's spirit is at work offering new insights and revelation for our daily living and decision making.

What follows is a general description of how a small-group process might be structured. You know your own context best, so feel free to adapt as needed.

Theological Reflection in a Small Group

Large community gatherings such as worship or a sports event or a night-school class can be stimulating. However, a small group offers a different kind of experience because there is space to speak and to develop a sense of belonging. Offering thoughts and feelings is easier in a small group than in a larger gathering. A group of respectful listeners offers a supportive environment to share life struggles. When a group blends well, it can be time to build close community, and a sense of belonging emerges. This kind of group can offer a supportive situation in which to explore our faith and our baptismal call to ministry. Our call from God is both a private experience and a communal experience through affirmation within a faith community. While we may feel a sense of God's presence in our hearts, it is deeply satisfying to have others recognize and confirm God's spirit at work in our lives. Sometimes our faith community sees gifts in us that we did not know we had. One person summed up the experience of a theological reflection group by saying, "I always assumed that ministry was what ordained people did. I've discovered that as a layperson, I have a ministry too."

Theological Reflection: Nuts and Bolts

Theological reflection is simply wondering about God's activity in our lives. Where is God present? What is God calling us to do? By taking time to ask questions about what happens to us, seeing our experiences through the lens of faith, we become clearer about our connection to God. We all ask questions about relationships, our work, our children, our government, and our situation in life. We all reflect, wonder, analyze, think, assess, and discuss with friends, as ways of trying to understand our life. Theological reflection simply refocuses all that thinking to encourage a stronger sense of relationship with God, asking, "Where does God fit into the picture?"

In the process I outline on pages 62-63, theological reflection has seven steps:

Step 1 identifies an event or situation on which to reflect. While this event can come from any part of our lives, it is more effective to deal with a situation that is current and still has some fresh feelings attached. Situations that are already resolved offer fewer possibilities for new insights. Also, deeper, unresolved issues from our past may need more intense debriefing from a spiritual director or counselor than is possible in a congregational small group.

Step 2 asks us to name and describe our feelings about the situation. You may be feeling joy or frustration, sadness or anger, energy or boredom. All feelings are worth including in this process and sharing with God—the God who knows us intimately, the God from whom we cannot hide, who loves us and accepts all that we are. With God, we need not fear sharing whatever feelings are whirling around a particular event. And in a supportive group, sharing our feelings can be an affirming experience. Sometimes we find that other people have similar feelings, making us realize that we are not alone.

Identifying feelings is easy for some and more difficult for others. Asking ourselves what challenged, stimulated, or disturbed us is another way to get at the question of feelings. Try to keep "feeling" sentences simple, saying, "I feel sad" or "I feel angry" or "I feel joy." As soon as you add other words,

Reflecting with God

1. Naming the Experience: *Choosing an Event on Which to Reflect*

Choose an event, a moment, a conversation, or a situation. As you recall the event, ask yourself:
- What happened?
- Who was involved?
- What did you do or say?

2. Exploring the Experience: *Finding Another Layer to the Event*

To explore another layer in this event, ask yourself:
- How did you feel?
- What challenged, stimulated, or disturbed you?
- What was happening for others in the situation?

3. Digging Deeper: *Expanding Your Thinking*

To discover another layer of reflection, ask yourself:
- What do you think about the situation?
- What core values emerge as you think about this event?
- What values are different from yours?
- What social issues, power issues, or economic issues are at work?

4. Making Faith Connections: *Finding God at Work in This Event*

To make faith connections, ask yourself:
- Where is God present for you in this situation?
- Where is God present for others?
- Does this event remind you of a Scripture passage, a hymn, or other resources from your faith tradition?
- What theological issues or themes are present?
- What traditions of our church speak to this situation?
- Are you affirmed or challenged in your present actions or beliefs?

5. Learning: *Naming Your Discoveries*

To draw out what you learned, ask yourself:
- What questions still linger?
- Were you challenged to change present actions or beliefs?
- What have you learned about yourself?
- What have you learned about God?
- What do you need?
- What will you do now?

6. Praying: *Taking Time with God*

To conclude your reflection, write a prayer emerging from this event.

7. Presenting to the Group: *Preparing for Group Discussion*

Present your written reflection to the group by reading it aloud. This reading will be followed by group discussion. As you think about the discussion time, how would you like the group to focus? Discussion is not a problem-solving exercise but a way to extend your personal reflection. Here are some suggestions to focus the group discussion:
- Is there a question still lingering for which you would like group wisdom?
- Do you want group members to share their experiences with a similar situation?
- Do you want to hear group members' thoughts about further theological or biblical connections?
- Do you want to know where others see God at work?

then you are moving into thinking rather than feeling. For example, "I feel that . . ." shifts away from what you are feeling into statements and opinions. If I have had a difficult conversation with a colleague I might express my feelings by saying "I feel angry when my colleague criticizes my work because I really tried my best." Using the formula "I feel —— when —— because ——" keeps my feelings clear. As soon as I use the word *that*, I shift away from my feelings, saying, for example, "I feel that my colleague was unfair in criticizing my work because I did the best I could." While this second sentence conveys a similar idea, I have not examined my feelings about the issue. I have simply shifted the focus to my colleague.

Knowing how we feel is an important part of the reflective process but not the only part. Sorting through feelings allows us to acknowledge and recognize what we feel but makes it distinct from what we think and how we behave. For instance, I feel frustrated and angry dealing with a toddler who is a having a temper tantrum. I am entitled to my feelings of frustration and anger, but I also need to think about the dynamics involved. As an adult and a parent, I am a responsible person and need to keep the toddler safe. I need also to be clear that my behavior is distinct from my feelings; otherwise, I might end up lashing out at the toddler and later regretting my actions.

Taking time to identify feelings helps us to sort out what is going on internally as we reflect on an event. In addition, being clear about my own feelings helps me to be aware of others' feelings as distinct from my own. My feelings are not the only emotional activity in a situation, and reflecting on the sadness and joy of others helps to unpack what was going on. The fact that I feel sad does not mean that everyone feels sad about the same event. Understanding how others feel as distinct from how I feel may help me to see what motivates their behavior.

Step 3 offers an opportunity to explore what you think about the situation and what dynamics are at play. Various factors are involved in any event, from office politics to personality traits to the history leading up to the event. Thinking through these various dynamics brings further clarity to the situation and helps us to see the complexity involved. You may want to bring analytical tools to the situation, such as power analysis. Who has power in this situation? Who does not? You may want to use economic analysis or social analysis as you think through social justice issues at play in this event. You may have other analytical tools you use in your work situation. For instance, the parish nurse I mentioned earlier uses diagnostic tools to assess a situation and to think through what is going on. Exploring what we think about a situation gives us some distance from the immediate feelings that arise, so that we can move on to the next steps.

Step 4 invites us to connect with God, to ask where God is present in our chosen situation. Begin by asking yourself where God is at work. Think about a biblical story or biblical text that has a connection to the event. You may have a faith stance that informs the situation. For instance, in dealing with my difficult toddler, my faith tells me that he is a dearly loved child of God. He may be less dear to me in this stressful moment; but God knows the number of hairs on his head, and I can draw strength from a sense of God's presence and care. A Scripture passage that comes to mind is the account of Jesus' welcoming the children and blessing them despite the protests of the disciples. As I watch my toddler screaming and beating his hands and feet on the floor, I feel like a protesting disciple, but Jesus' action reminds me that each child is blessed and loved. In addition, when we think about our faith connection, we can draw on other resources such as hymns, creeds, liturgy, and writings of the church. For instance, one person reflected on his service club's involvement with bingo as a fund-raising event. He used a church document on gambling to reflect theologically on this issue.

Step 5 asks us to think about what we have learned from this reflection. We may have gained some insights. We may

decide on some new action. Perhaps we will do something differently next time, or we may feel a deeper conviction about
what we have done. Usually, I have a different perspective on
the situation by step 5 than when I began at step 1.

Step 6 invites us to pray. In one sense, the whole reflection
process is prayer, because it is intentional quiet time when we
are conscious of God's presence in our lives. Yet concluding
with an explicit prayer draws our whole reflection into an expression of our deepest hope. It takes all our hurts and joys, all
insights and lingering questions into an intimate conversation
with God. I have found that people using this process as a
personal spiritual journey have deepened their prayer life or
sometimes even *discovered* a prayer life if they had not experienced one before. It also takes the process of reflection from
the posture of thinking about God to one of being with God.

Step 6 ends our personal reflective process and brings us to
step 7—presenting to the group. Or, if you are using "Reflecting with God" as a personal spiritual journey, you may want to
use the group preparation section as a focus for time with a
mentor.

The situations that people choose are varied. Some events
are relatively simple and easy to sort through: something happened, we worked through what took place using the reflective questions, and we feel a sense of resolution. In other
situations, we might come back to a similar event again and
again throughout our lives. For instance, each time I experience a death in my life, this experience raises questions for me.
When I was 12 and my grandfather died, I began for the first
time to think about life and death and where people go after
they die. In my emerging faith, I had a sense of heaven, but
now began to imagine in more detail how that place might
look. In my later teen years, when an elderly aunt died, I did
not want to imagine heaven, because the idea of heaven felt
too childish, but I did wonder about other faiths and belief
systems—imagining, for example, what reincarnation might be

like. In still later years, in my work as the minister of a congregation, I have meditated more deeply on theological questions of death, dying, and life after death. Each death is unique. The death of an older person who has lived a rich and substantial life is different from the death of a child. As you can see, with this profound example, some issues or situations occur over and over again, offering an opportunity to deepen our reflection and our faith.

Theological reflection is not a problem-solving process. Reflection is an open-ended process, with no right or wrong answers. Clear answers may not emerge, and we may not find quick fixes to life's problems; yet we will find deeper meaning through conversation with God about everyday issues. Theological reflection is an opportunity to deepen a sense of God's presence in our lives, and an opportunity to discover what we believe and how our faith and life intersect. Typically, I find that many questions come to mind as I reflect on a situation. Rather than seeking answers, I try to "live the questions" as I discern where God is leading me, being attentive to God's voice in my life and work.

Getting Stuck

As people begin to use these models, they will find sticking points or places where they get stuck in their process of reflection. This place will be different for each person. For instance, someone who is a keen thinker may find it hard to put down his or her feelings on paper, whereas a "feeling person" will find it hard to do analysis. Another person may get so engrossed in the detail of describing the event that he or she gets lost in the details and finds it hard to move on to feeling and thinking. Some people find it hard to name where God is present in their lives. As facilitator, assure people that this kind of reflection is a learning process. Suggest that they write what they can and gently push at those sticking points as time goes by.

For someone new to theological reflection, it may take time to feel comfortable with the process. As when one exercises for the first time, unused muscles will protest. With persistence, muscles develop strength and tone. Gently encourage people to develop strength by awakening those reflective and spiritual muscles.

Whether you use "Reflecting with God" as a personal spiritual journey or in a small-group process, I strongly recommend that you do it as a written exercise. A different attitude takes hold when you commit your thoughts to paper. The very action of putting pen to paper or seeing words form on a computer screen creates a pause in our lives in which to reflect, to find meaning in what took place, to understand what happened more deeply, and to transform those events in our lives. Writing or typing helps us to step back into the event, yet distance is created through writing that allows for thoughtful response rather than impulsive reaction. In the struggle to put our thoughts and feelings into words on a page, we can find new clarity and insight. People can choose the writing method that suits them best. Some people have a special journal and prefer to write by hand. Others keep a computer file of the "Reflecting with God" questions, with space between to add their responses. Still others run off several printed copies of "Reflecting with God," with space between questions so that they can add their thoughts in point form by hand. Use whatever method works for you.

From Reflection to Conversation

As outlined in chapter 3, after the initial meetings where people share a little of their life stories and get to know one another, subsequent meetings focus on an individual "Reflecting with God" presentation. All group members sign up for a meeting at which it will be their turn to offer a presentation. Before that meeting, each person will have taken time to reflect on a situation using the "Reflecting with God" questions. Reflections need to be in written form to keep the presenter on track and undistracted by the temptation to add further description or explanation. A presenter simply reads what he or she has written. Handing out copies of the written presentation is helpful, as some group members may be visual learners, and some may have trouble hearing. All group members would benefit from seeing a printed copy. These copies can be handed back to the presenter at the end of the meeting. After a presentation, the group has an opportunity for discussion, focusing on questions raised by the presenter.

Presentation of Theological Reflection

A presenter may be a little nervous in sharing private thoughts with the group. Many people have not been in an environment where feelings, thoughts, and faith issues are discussed. Encouragement from the facilitator is important in calming nerves and creating a respectful atmosphere. Nonetheless, even though people may be nervous, I find that they are excited to share with others and look forward to group input and discussion.

Once a presenter has finished reading the presentation and offering focus questions for discussion, he or she can take a deep breath and relax. Now the group gets to work. Once the focus questions are offered to the group, the facilitator takes initiative for the next step of group discussion, allowing the presenter to sit quietly and listen. A presenter must resist the impulse to add more detail or to jump in and talk at great length about the issue. Sitting quietly is part of a spiritual discipline; one offers the situation to God's Holy Spirit and practices "deep listening." Like prayer, presenting and then sitting quietly symbolize a time for speaking to God and a time of listening for God. The group becomes a gathering in which God's voice can be heard. God's spirit works in this small community to demonstrate and feel where the divine presence and activity are felt.

Group Discussion

After the presentation, ask group members if they have questions. There may have been words or ideas in the presentation that they did not understand. Take care that the questioners are not simply wanting more detail or beginning to try to fix the problem. If people begin by saying, "Did you think of . . . ?" or "You could have tried . . . ?" or "What if you had . . . ?" then the group is moving into fixing.

One important caution: The group discussion is not an opportunity to solve the presented problem or to psychologize about what is happening in a person's life. Discussion offers an opportunity for a small faith community to gather in reflection, focusing on where members see God at work in the person's life. Your role as facilitator is to assist the flow of conversation. If the group begins to ask more questions of the presenter or begins to make suggestions about how to fix the problem, the facilitator can gently intervene, reminding people that this period is for making faith connections, not for solving the problem. This distinction is further enhanced if the presenter sits quietly during the ensuing discussion and listens, benefiting from hearing the wisdom of the group rather than interjecting further information or defensive responses. The group needs to trust that the presenter has the resources to find a solution to his or her own problem. The task of the group is to reflect on where God is at work and to stay focused on the questions the presenter has asked.

After the time for questions, take a brief break. Aside from an opportunity to get a drink or visit the facilities, it is a time to let what has been heard sink in. Encourage people not to discuss the issue until the group reconvenes. More introverted people have a moment to think and gather their thoughts before speaking. Extroverts want to get into discussion immediately, but it does not hurt to wait a few minutes.

Once the group reconvenes, remind everyone, "We are not here to solve the problem. Joe is competent and resourceful and will find his own way toward a solution. We are here to reflect on the faith issues, finding biblical connections and naming where we see God at work." Use questions the presenter has offered to focus discussion.

As mentioned in chapter 2, when time for discussion draws to a close, move to a time of reflecting on how people experienced their time together. Ask the group what has been helpful or unhelpful about the time together. You could begin by asking the presenter what he or she learned or found helpful in presenting to the group and listening to the discussion. Sometimes a time of silence, or a brief prayer, allows the group to shift gears from the stimulating discussion to a reflection on the whole experience of the meeting.

In Relationship with God

Theological reflection is an experiential process of growing and learning together in community. It has similarities to prayer: only by praying do we know how to pray. We could talk about prayer for a long time and be no clearer about how to pray. Through prayer we have a relationship with God rather than simply thinking about God. Similarly, with theological reflection, jump right in and begin the experience. The process of reflection is a conversation with God rather than an exercise to complete. As closeness and intimacy develop within the group, a sense of sacred time and space deepens, a space where faith, doubts, and wondering can be shared. I invite you to begin the reflection process. God waits breathlessly.

5

Wrinkles in the Fabric

WHEN MY FAMILY GETS TOGETHER, we usually have a great time catching up with one another, discussing local and global politics, and eating wonderful food. Along with these positive aspects are other characteristics of our time together: misunderstandings, arguments, and disagreements. Both the great times and the disagreements form the fabric of our lives together. While it would be wonderful to laugh and not to argue, to share our lives and not to have disagreements, we have learned that wrinkles are a normal part of our family life. Differences, conflict, and tension can be stressful to deal with, yet they indicate that people are willing to be authentic with one another and to share what they think and feel. This authenticity is essential to building intimate relationships.

Like family life, group life has its own combination of joy in being together and wrinkles in the fabric of joy. In this chapter, we will look at the wrinkles within the fabric of group life that are a normal part of being in relationship. Not only are these wrinkles normal; they are essential to developing greater intimacy. However, we need not stay in a place of tension, because we can work through it as a group. Working through the tension brings greater insight into how

73

each of us functions and how others are similar to and different from ourselves.

Group life has three aspects that need attention: individual needs, group needs, and the task of theological reflection. When a group attends to all three areas, each person feels valued, the group runs smoothly, and substantial learning through theological reflection takes place. If group time is taken up with addressing the needs of one individual, then time for the task of theological reflection is shortened. If the group focuses on the task of theological reflection but ignores the needs of individuals or of the group as a whole, then closeness may not develop within the group and significant sharing may not take place.

The group process outlined in previous chapters attempts to balance all three aspects of group life. If you are a new facilitator, you will need to make a concerted effort to maintain that balance. As with learning to ride a bike, however, after practice and time that balance will become more natural. New facilitators will expend attention and energy until nurturing group life becomes second nature. In the following sections, I will focus on ways in which group life may be out of alignment and ways to find equilibrium.

Silence Is Golden

In my experience, most groups feel comfortable with a balance between silence and speaking. Unless group members have experience with meditation and prayer, most are not comfortable with too much silence. And likewise, while groups enjoy conversation, tension builds when one or two people monopolize group discussion, filling the air with only their words.

Let us consider silence for a moment. The phrase "silence is golden" is often used to describe blessed peace in the midst of noise and confusion. After a day of working in an office space when renovations are taking place next door, the silence washes over me like balm for my soul when everyone puts down the tools for the day. Aside from providing a break from noise, silence can be a blessing when it brings an opportunity for reflection and a time to check in with internal messages.

Silence can be an important part of prayer life, too. After offering thoughts to God, messages of thanksgiving and intercession, a time of silence makes space for God's voice to be heard. Being silent can be healing. When accompanying people in times of great crisis, no words will ease the pain. Sitting in prayerful silence can be a gift of comfort and grace.

However, not all silence feels like blessing. Silence can be used as a weapon to freeze people out, or it can carry anger and resentment. Silence can be used to withhold love and intimacy. Silence is hard to interpret because the reason for silence is not always known. Body language and facial expressions are our only clues to the reason for silence.

Silence offers groups a mixture of blessing and tension. Let us look first at aspects of silence as blessing. Because silence offers time for reflection, you will want to build in silence to encourage thoughtful reflection rather than immediate response. In the opening time, have a moment of silence for participants to gather their thoughts before offering or inviting a prayer. After check-in, have a moment of silence before proceeding to the "Reflecting with God" presentation, to give time for people to change gears from the activity of check-in to the activity of listening to the presentation. After the presentation, a brief break for personal reflection helps people to absorb what they have heard. And after the group discussion, take a moment of silence for people to reflect on the wrap-up question, "What has been helpful or unhelpful in our time together?" Again, this rhythm gives time for people to switch gears. Silence gives group members space to change their focus from the group discussion to the way the entire session has worked for them.

As well as blessing, silence can also bring tension. This silence may come from two sources: the group as a whole or

individuals. Either the group as a whole is quiet, or one or two
people say very little in comparison to others. When the group
as a whole is silent, this reaction may be normal for the context. Are they normally a quiet group? Is silence part of the
behavior of the larger community? Silence may be a normal
and even essential part of community life. For instance, in
Quaker services, members spend large amounts of gathering
time in silence until someone feels moved by God's spirit to
speak. If silence in a reflection group is normal, then you as
facilitator need to adjust to the rhythm of the group.

As facilitator, I have learned how to adapt myself to each
group's personality rather than setting hard-and-fast rules for
how they should behave. Preferring a quick oral response, I
have learned to sit quietly and wait for people to speak rather
than jumping in to fill the silence. As facilitator, be aware of
your own level of comfort with silence, and do not be too
quick to jump in to fill the gap.

Typically, in my experience, most worshiping communities and small groups are far from comfortable with silence. A
group's silence may signal discomfort. Do the participants need
time to absorb what they have heard? Are they unsure how to
begin discussion? Is there some tension that needs to be expressed? Allow a brief space for people to stay with what they
are feeling; then ask what is happening for them. Usually, within
a group each individual has a different reason for choosing to
be silent, so expect a variety of responses. Once you have heard
the reasons for the silence, you can address whatever issues are
expressed.

Silence may not be arising from the group as a whole, however, but from one or two individuals. Some people say very
little. As facilitator, think about what is happening. If the group
is very energetic and talkative, it may be hard for a quieter
person to get a word in. Also, some people need time to com-
pose their thoughts before offering anything to the group. If
someone is naturally shy or simply a quieter individual, then

the group can talk about ways of deliberately including this person in discussion. An invitation from time to time might be helpful. "We haven't heard from you, Sherry. Would you like to offer something?" However, sometimes an invitation puts people on the spot. One person in a group I worked with declared, "When I have something to say, I will say it." Not all invitations will be accepted.

Developing the group covenant in the first session is an opportunity to discuss ways for everyone to speak in the group. This discussion establishes group norms for sharing and encourages awareness of the need to create space for each person to speak. Another way to encourage space for everyone to speak is by offering a different format for giving input. For instance, during check-in, go around the circle of participants rather than waiting for people to jump in when they are ready. It speeds things up, and people know when their turn is coming. If someone has little to offer, he or she can say, "I'll pass this session." Or if people are not ready, they can say, "Come back to me at the end." Or, with check-in that has random input, ask people to be brief, allowing only 10 or 15 minutes for total check-in time. This limitation encourages brief responses rather than life stories.

Occasionally someone who usually speaks readily is silent, signaling a problem. A change in behavior often indicates that something has altered for the individual, whether positively or negatively. If a person has not offered any information during check-in about what is happening in her or his life, then the facilitator might want to follow up with that person after the group session.

In one instance, George was having problems with his teenage daughter that caused him a great deal of stress. He did not want to share that information with the group, because he wanted to respect the privacy of his daughter, yet the personal situation had changed the quality of his presence in the group. I suggested that during check-in he could say, "I am dealing with a stressful issue in my life that I am not able to talk about at this point. I appreciate the support and prayers of the group as I work through this and will do my best to be attentive in our sessions." A statement like this acknowledges to the group that something is wrong while respecting privacy and boundaries. The group probably intuited that George was not his usual self, but his clear declaration allowed group life and the task at hand to carry on.

While too much silence can bring tension, on the other end of the spectrum of human interaction too much talking can bring a different tension. If the whole group is outgoing and talkative, then one of the facilitator's primary tasks will be to keep the discussion focused on the topic at hand rather than allowing the group to wander off the subject, and to build in short times of silence to encourage reflection, as noted above. However, if one or two individuals talk too much, the facilitator's task changes.

For example, Ted was extremely talkative. He was always the first to respond. He had the most to say, and he interjected comments and responses after each person spoke. Depending on how assertive you are, you can speak to a person like Ted either quietly after a session or directly during a session. Being fairly assertive, I chose to speak to Ted immediately in the first session by saying, "Ted, you have a lot of interesting ideas to offer. I wonder whether you could hold on to some of them, so that others have a chance to contribute." After the session, I checked in with Ted about how he felt trying a quieter role in the group. He acknowledged that he tended to talk a lot and that perhaps listening more would be helpful. In addition, the discipline of going around the circle at check-in helped Ted learned how to listen without needing to respond to each person. A few times, Ted asked me how he was doing with being quieter in the group. We began to talk in some depth about his need to talk so much. Others had given him similar feedback in other settings, so he was interested in addressing this behavior. This small-group interaction encouraged Ted to become more self-aware and to reflect on personal issues that were fueling his behavior.

Ted is an extreme case, however. Typically, the group covenant raises people's awareness of sharing conversational space enough to prevent anyone from dominating. Also, the wrap-up time at the end of each session offers an opportunity to attend to group dynamics, such as whether everyone has had a chance to say what needs to be said.

Paying attention to your own comfort with silence as well as attention to how the group deals with silence is an important part of your role. Your own level of comfort with silence will directly affect how well you are able to ensure that everyone in the group has space to share. In addition, an awareness of how much we speak and how participants fill the air with the sounds of their own voices come at the other end of the conversational spectrum. Balancing time for good discussion and for silence is part of the art of facilitation.

Conflict

Depending on how conflict was dealt with in our families and depending on our own conflict style, we may be more or less comfortable with this area of group life. I assume that conflict is a normal part of all human interactions. Nonetheless, some types of conflictive behavior are easier to deal with than others. As part of family life, I prefer a forthright sharing of feelings and thoughts with all parties committed to finding a solution. I do not like name-calling, temper tantrums, and shouting. Other family members like to have a good fight with lots of theatrics, floods of tears called "a good cry," and a cathartic act of making up to round everything off. As a family, we have learned how to deal with the differences in our conflict behaviors and styles, although this learning is an ongoing process.

In a group, each person brings his or her own conflict styles and preferences from a unique family background. Some people prefer peace at any cost; their style may be avoidance. Some people have a more persuasive style and feel compelled to convert others to their point of view. Others with an assertive style simply like to wade into an argument and get excited when a discussion heats up. When developing the group covenant in the first session, talk about how the group would like to deal with conflict.

In the annotated bibliography, I mention excellent resources to explore the topic of conflict in more depth. In addition, Marlene Wilson, in her book on managing church volunteers, suggests a helpful approach to conflict within groups and congregations.* She highlights four levels of conflict and how they may be addressed. A first level of conflict is informational. People do not have the same information, and a simple exchange of facts and sharing of conflicting viewpoints is sufficient to clear up any misunderstanding. A second level of conflict occurs when people disagree about how things are to be done. Brainstorming or problem solving is a good approach that encourages input on how the group might proceed.

At the third level of conflict, differences are evident in why we do things the way we do. This level needs more attention and may require a time apart for deeper discussion, or an outside mediator. At the fourth level of conflict, dearly held ideals, beliefs, and values are in opposition. This can be the most difficult area of disagreement and requires finding common ground before proceeding. In my experience, theological reflection groups rarely get to levels three and four because the reasons for our involvement in the group and the underlying assumptions about the group and its process are clearly laid out at the beginning. Certainly a variety of theological view-

---

*Marlene Wilson, *How to Mobilize Church Volunteers* (Minneapolis: Augsburg, 1983).

points will be represented, so encouraging an environment of respectful sharing that assumes theological differences addresses the possibility of fourth-level conflict.

Typically, groups get bogged down in level 1 and 2 conflict. Level 1 is easily addressed by clarifying information. Level 2 needs a little more attention. For example, Stella had become very frustrated because she thought another member of the group, Alex, needed to claim a lot of the group's attention. When Stella finally expressed her views, because she felt that Alex was getting in the way of group discussion, Alex was understandably upset. He wanted to know whether others felt the same way. Feedback from others indicated that they had observed a similar pattern in Alex but had not reacted as strongly as Stella had. After hearing the feedback, Alex wanted time to think things through, so the group agreed to come back to the matter at the next meeting. When the group met again, Alex apologized for monopolizing group time and energy and said he wanted to try to be more attentive to his interaction in the group. Stella also apologized for hurting Alex but added that she thought that for the life of the group, she had to name her feelings. Once Alex and Stella had spoken, group members decided they did not want to discuss the issue further and wanted to move on with the theological reflection. Nothing more was said in the group about the matter. Alex indeed became more sensitive about how he used group time, and Stella was pleased that there was improvement, but learned to let go of her frustration with Alex. Learning to live with our differences is a reality of family and community living.

Usually, a facilitator mediates discussion to find a common ground of understanding or simply to help people agree to disagree. However, in extreme cases, if conflict moves to another level and differences become too intense and beyond the skill of the facilitator to resolve, then an outside mediator can be helpful in working through the issues. A wise and trusted person who is experienced in conflict mediation and comfortable with group processes is ideal. In my experience, an outside mediator is rarely needed, but being prepared for this possibility can make it easier for us to deal with whatever might happen.

If you are a new facilitator, beyond writing in your journal as a reflection tool, think about finding someone with whom you can check in about the progress of group life and about facilitation issues that come up. Because I am a teacher, my students often ask me questions about different group dynamics that arise in their ministry placements. Thinking through various possibilities is helpful preparation but cannot cover all the issues that spontaneously arise. Facilitation is a spontaneous art, and being able to respond in the moment and being creative on the spot are important skills.

An interesting image for facilitation is jazz improvisation. A jazz musician has learned all kinds of scales and arpeggios and pieces of music, all carefully practiced and rehearsed. The moment of improvisation is a spontaneous collage, incorporating pieces of all that has been learned previously to create something entirely new in response to a particular musical moment.

Group facilitation is similar to jazz improvisation in that it is a spontaneous, creative process, drawing on life experience and personal and interpersonal dynamics to respond and create something new within the moment. Facilitators do not need a briefcase full of right answers as much as they need the creativity to respond to a variety of situations. Later, there will be time to reflect theologically on what took place, and in that reflection, greater wisdom will emerge.

For many of us, conflict is not a comfortable aspect of group life. However, conflict is a normal part of human interaction. In small-group life, we have an opportunity to respond to God's call to faithful living. As Christians, we are called to love one another, not just our friends or those people we get along with, but all people. Loving one another does not mean sentimental love that tolerates all behavior. It does mean being authentically in community, respectfully offering and receiving different points of view and ways of being. We are trying to be faithful through reflecting theologically on our lives, and we are trying to be faithful in our relationships with one another in the group. Both living together and reflecting on how we live together are part of what it means to be faithful disciples.

Difficult People

Every time the Bible study group met, Joe faithfully attended. He was not really interested in reading the Bible, even though he carried a large Bible with him everywhere he went. He was not interested in group discussion in which each person offered his or her understanding of a biblical text. According to Joe, only one thing mattered: Jesus Christ died to save us from our sins, and we all need to repent and ask to be saved. Gently, people would suggest that while they respected his views, they did not share them. Unfortunately, Joe was unable to listen to any view except his own. He would reiterate that holding a different viewpoint was a matter of life and death. We would all die and would not enjoy the grace of life after death. Because Joe was clearly not open to engaging in biblical reflection or in learning from the group, I asked him, with sadness, not to come back again. Joe's theology was not the stumbling block for the group. I asked Joe to leave because he was unable to be open to other viewpoints and to accept an open format for discussion.

In general, every group has limits of inclusion. While we might wish to include everyone, the purpose or structure of the group may limit whom we make room for. The intent or purpose of some groups may automatically create an exclusive group. For instance, I belonged to a women's self-defense group that wanted to provide a safe environment for women. Many of them had experienced sexual assault or abuse. This group had set a boundary: it was for women only. In our congregations we may also have groups that have clear boundaries. One congregation where I served enjoyed a vital men's group that met for breakfast once a month. My predecessor, a male minister, had been a welcome member. I could have attended this group in my role as minister, but I respected the need for a men's discussion and spirituality group and chose not to attend unless invited for special events open to all.

While we may agree or disagree with boundaries that have been set up for various groups, at least those boundaries are clear. When boundaries are unclear, however, problems occur. In Joe's case, while the Bible study group wanted to include everyone, there were implicit group norms that made Joe's presence difficult. These group norms could have been made clear in a group covenant. Generally in our society we err on the side of caution and politeness, partly to keep the peace and partly to respect the feelings of others. However, a group has limits to what it can tolerate. When the disruption of one individual causes a breakdown in group dynamics and an inability to proceed with the task, then a facilitator must address the disruptive individual.

As facilitator, you might begin by naming the problem directly with the individual. Group members spoke clearly but gently to Joe about how they were experiencing his assertive approach. When he did not pay attention to group members, I had a one-on-one conversation with him and described the intent of the group and the way the process of open conversation occurred. Joe strongly disagreed with the process. When I asked him why he was attending the group, since it did not seem to meet his needs, he was clear. His agenda was to save the group. Again, his theology was not at issue. Rather, the issue was the way he chose to impose his views on the group. Joe chose not to respect the group norms, so it became clear that I would have to ask him to leave.

Asking someone to leave a group may be the hardest thing a facilitator has to do. In my experience, it rarely happens. On the other hand, when an individual is extremely disruptive to group life and will not honor agreed-upon group norms, then a facilitator has to take the initiative by asking the person to leave the group.

Theological Reflection or Therapy?

From time to time, a person offers a theological reflection presentation that is clearly about a major personal or psychological crisis in his or her life. Such a presentation raises a tension between theological reflection and group therapy. First, this group is not intended to be group therapy or group counseling. Second, being a group facilitator is not the same as being a group therapist.

While people bring substantial issues from their lives to their theological reflection presentation, the emphasis is on seeking God in the midst of this experience rather than looking for therapeutic responses from the group. This kind of group is not intended to deal with major crises in people's lives. Group members may be sympathetic and can offer prayer and support, but when a person experiences a major psychological crisis, drawing on others with specialized skills is essential. The difference between the needs appropriately presented in theological reflection and those that require therapy is like the difference between cutting my finger on a kitchen knife and having a life-threatening artery gash. In the first instance, I may want the attention of a supportive group and some Band-Aids and prayer. In the second instance, I need people with specialized skills, such as paramedics, nurses, and doctors, to save my life— not well-intentioned group members. The difference is one of degree, not the nature of the issue being discussed. That is not to say that people going through crises cannot be part of the group, but it does mean that they may need to discern what to share with the group. Again, using the medical example, a person who has had a heart attack has relied on skilled doctors and nurses to deal with the immediate crisis but may reflect theologically about the experience of the heart attack with the group.

As facilitator, your role is not to offer group therapy. Unless you have counseling or therapeutic skills, you are not equipped to play this role. Even if you do have those skills, therapy is not the intent of the group. A therapist is concerned with the mental health and healing of individuals within a group. A facilitator's role is to encourage conversation and discussion. As facilitator, part of your role is to distinguish between theological reflection and group therapy. As mentioned in chapter 3, at times you will need to prevent the group from jumping in to fix problems or to psychologize the issues presented. Reflection time with your journal or with a more experienced group facilitator can help to frame this distinction, because at times the lines can seem a little fuzzy.

Typically, as each person uses the "Reflecting with God" format, he or she will be asked to address personal feelings near the beginning of the reflection. When a person has thought through various issues in the situation, feelings are not as raw or intense as they might be in a therapy session. The individual will have moved through feelings to analysis and faith connections. Sometimes a presenter will come to me to discuss whether to present certain issues. Most of us are working through all sorts of issues, so it is generally not necessary to present one fraught with trauma to experience growth from the theological reflection experience.

However, there have been times when someone has presented a crisis that goes beyond the scope and ability of the group. As facilitators, we have clear responsibilities. We do not want people to feel alone in dealing with difficult issues, or ashamed for bringing them to the group. The task at this point is to help the person recognize that the issue is one that the group does not have the skills to address and to set clear boundaries and discuss how the person can find the resources needed to deal with the situation.

For example, in one group I worked with, a mother offered a reflection in which she was grappling with a case of child sexual abuse involving her daughter and her estranged husband. Her daughter had revealed that her father was touching her in places that made her uncomfortable. In this instance, my responsibility was clearly to act on behalf of the child by informing authorities. This was not a situation for general group discussion on the issue presented, so I stated that we would not be proceeding with the usual format for discussion. Instead, we took time to outline an action plan with the mother, and we prayed for all concerned. Theological reflection was not appropriate at this point. At a later time, when clear issues had been addressed, such as finding care for the child and support for the mother, then reflection on where God had been present would be appropriate. In the immediate moment, God was a god of action, working for justice and safety for a child and a mother in need.

In another case, Doug spoke in his presentation about his ongoing struggle with depression over a 10-year period. However, he was seeing a therapist, used medication when needed to deal with particularly difficult low times, and had a supportive family. He wanted to reflect with the group on how depression is a hidden disease, as well as to point to some of the stigmas attached to mental illness. His theological reflection presentation stimulated a fruitful discussion as everyone reflected on God's care of those with mental illness. Biblical stories of healing were named, such as the one about the man from Gerasene who was possessed by demons. In addition, group members talked about their struggle to pray for healing when healing does not happen. In this situation, theological reflection, rather than therapy, took place, even though the situation raised deeply personal issues and feelings. The difference was that we were not attempting to fix Doug's depression or to deal with an immediate crisis that needed specialized attention. Instead, we were seeking to find where God was at work in Doug's life and discovering more about God's relationship to each one of us.

As with other areas of group life, I am offering examples that rarely happen, yet it helps to be prepared when they do. If we dealt with crisis as a regular part of our day—for instance, as a critical-care nurse—we would have routine procedures for dealing with crisis. Because the situations I am naming happen rarely, we do not immediately know how to respond. I do not intend to make you nervous by painting worst-case scenarios when most groups are friendly, cooperative, productive, and successful. However, I do want to offer clear tools for flexible and responsive facilitation when challenges arise.

Facilitation as an Art

Perhaps the best way to summarize this chapter is to say that facilitation is an art. It requires tools for engaging a group in conversation with one another through theological reflection. It requires forethought and planning. Yet no matter how well prepared we are, the need for creative, spontaneous improvisation in the moment elevates the task of the facilitator to an art form.

One element of this art form is our own personalities. Good facilitators have a strong self-awareness. They know themselves well. They know their strengths and their cutting edges, what excites them and what hot buttons set them off. Knowing ourselves well means that we will not use the group to meet our own needs for attention, status, or love. Instead, we will find what we need outside the group, so that we can be clear and attentive to the needs of individuals and of the group to encourage everyone in the task of theological reflection.

In addition, knowing ourselves well means that we can bring our unique gifts to our task. For instance, I mentioned earlier that I am fairly assertive. I am able to name issues that come up in a group to encourage insight and discussion. Others may not feel comfortable with that style of leadership. I once worked with Bob as a co-facilitator. Bob offered a very different style of leadership from mine in his laid-back, gentle approach. We worked well together, because we offered complementary styles. Neither was right nor wrong; each style brought a different dynamic to the group. On the other hand, at times my forthright approach felt heavy-handed, whereas Bob's gentle, more oblique approach suited the moment. Likewise, his gentle approach at times felt too timid when a more robust response was needed. Over the years, I have found that I need to use my innate gifts of leadership as well as to develop a variety of styles to meet the moment. While I can be assertive I have learned, and will continue to learn, how to offer a gentler approach. I find I have to work hardest at the attributes of which I have the least. However, I believe I have grown in wisdom and balance as a result.

As a facilitator, reflect on your style. What are the distinctive gifts of personality that you bring to group leadership? When will those gifts be most appreciated? What areas will you need to work on? How can you be mindful about trying new ways of offering leadership? Use your journal to do this reflection, and keep a log of both your gifts and those areas you are working on. You may also want to check with others about what gifts they see in you, because sometimes the characteristics we like least about ourselves are some of our greatest gifts. And the things we think are our greatest gifts sometimes do not sit well with others. Also, our gifts are not always obvious to us. We may believe that everyone can do what we do so easily.

Facilitation is an art and a vocation. God calls forth our gifts of leadership, blessing us with distinctive styles and encouraging us to hone new skills. We are accountable to God for the care of each individual and for the whole life of the group. We are not alone in our work. Through prayer, theological reflection, and supportive conversation with wise mentors, we can offer leadership that encourages others to reflect on their life of faith. Like a weaver, we will help others take the threads of their lives and create a fabric that will more clearly depict the face of God.

6

Outward Ripples

A STONE TOSSED INTO A POND SINKS to the bottom unseen, yet outward ripples on the surface of the water demonstrate the lingering effect of the stone's impact. Likewise, the lingering effect of small groups engaging in theological reflection makes an impact on the ongoing life of a congregation. A congregation is organic; what happens in one aspect of congregational life affects other aspects.

Layers of Belonging

Over 20 years ago, Ann Weems,* a writer and workshop leader, wrote a dialogue that identifies our inner yearning for belonging, to know one another more intimately and to be known by others. Both people in the dialogue verbalize a silent mental conversation that takes place during a worship service as each wonders about the other, while they are seated side by side in the pew. Each wonders what the other is thinking and feeling. Why do you come to church? Do you participate in church

---

*Ann Weems, "You—Sitting in the Pew Next to Me," in *Reaching for Rainbows: Resources for Creative Worship* (Philadelphia: Westminster, 1980), 51-56.

activities for fun, or do you find a deeper meaning? Each expresses an inner longing, unspoken to the pew neighbor. Do you know that I am lonely? Do you know that my life is changing? As the service comes to an end, their inner reverie is interrupted. They turn to each other with a bland greeting and a comment about the weather. This provocative dialogue highlights our curiosity about one another and our desire to be in intimate community. However, barriers of social convention, shyness, and lack of time or appropriate context prevent us moving from superficial conversation into more meaningful interaction.

Being part of a faith community offers opportunities to deepen a sense of God's presence through the gathered community. One important factor in experiencing God's presence is a sense of belonging. People feel they belong to a faith community when they are recognized and known by name, when they feel they are making a contribution to the community, and when their experiences, thoughts, and feelings are valued. Faith communities are not always good at creating an environment that encourages feelings of belonging. However, they have a mission and mandate to provide a hospitable place for both members and strangers.

Our mission and mandate comes from God and Jesus Christ. God invites us into a covenant relationship. God knows us personally, even intimately, and has called us by name and numbered the hairs on our head. God knows our joy and our hopelessness. God celebrates when we are joyful and weeps with us when we feel the despair of abandonment. Believing that this powerful and intimate love is freely offered to me, I need to realize that this love is offered to all people, those people whom I love and those I do not like or those I consider to be my enemies. This immense love of God for humanity challenges the way we are in relationship with one another. In knowing that God loves me so deeply, I am called to love others in the same way, to attempt to see others as God sees them.

God's call to love others is not just an invitation to a lovefest within our faith communities; it calls us into relationship in our local communities, our nation, and around the globe. In addition, God calls us to be partners in caring for creation through teaching, healing, being good stewards of the environment, and seeking justice for all. God's way of being in relationship with creation defines what it means for us to be in relationship with one another as an intimate, personal, and accountable community.

Similarly, Jesus lived God's call to relationship through his ministry. He recognized and knew by name those who had long been marginalized in society and in religious communities. He called people by name to make a contribution to the lives of others. Being called by Jesus was not a sentimental journey. He was demanding in that he expected people to grow in their relationship with God, to repent of sinful ways of living, and to show God's love to all through teaching, preaching, and healing. Jesus expected a great deal from his followers, yet his love was so transforming that people were willing to offer their lives to follow him.

Belonging and Theological Reflection

A sense of belonging is a fundamental aspect of life in a faith community. In congregations small or large, offering opportunities to be in small groups for discussion and support is an essential part of creating an environment of belonging. Many resources are available to explore small-group ministries that offer Christian education, personal support, and development, as well as interpersonal exploration.

In this book I have focused on one dimension of small-group ministry—theological reflection. Through the process outlined, this small group becomes a microcosm of the larger congregation by offering a greater sense of belonging. People get to know one another in a way they typically do not experience in congregational committee structures. In a small group, everyone is known by name. Sharing daily joys and frustrations in a respectful environment validates group members' feelings and thoughts, particularly about spiritual experiences of God.

And most important, this group is bound in covenant with one another and with God. As people talk about their daily experiences with one another, God surrounds the conversation. God is a listening partner. God becomes the lens through which people see their lives anew. God becomes the ear through which we listen to one another with compassion, understanding, and accountability. Within this small group, we belong to one another, and we belong to God.

Some groups may want to continue the process of gathering to do theological reflection throughout the year or to meet only for the number of sessions needed for everyone to present a reflection. The length of time for meeting is up to the group and the facilitator. I prefer a short-term commitment. Our lives are so busy and complicated that a short-term commitment seems easier to manage in today's congregations. Also, while groups develop a deep level of intimacy as sharing takes place from session to session, they need to return to lives that are not as strongly embedded with one another. I liken these groups to experiences of summer camp where everyone lives together, sharing mutual experiences of sunburn, mosquito bites, capsized canoes, campfires, and tent living. Enjoying the experience, no one wants to leave the deep friendships formed when camp comes to an end. However, when we return to our normal routines, the intimacy of camp falls into perspective. It is only one part of our lives, not our whole life. We need the ebb and flow of moving toward each other for intimacy and moving away from each other for perspective. We can always return to camp next summer.

Likewise, we can always join another theological reflection group when the opportunity is offered again. This way, we can get to know another group of people. Staying with the same group over a longer duration offers the advantage of deepening relationships, but it presents the possible drawback of the group's becoming a clique. In addition, it may be hard for people to withdraw from the group if there is no predetermined ending. Whether short- or long-term, set a clear ending date or a time to review continuation.

Short-term sessions build layers of belonging within the whole community. As group after group gathers for theological reflection, more and more people are learning about each other. Not only will we know about our families and our work and our community commitments; we will know about the strengths and doubts of our faith. Being known in this way gives us a place to celebrate our joys and to find support in our struggles.

Usually within most relationships we form, we share dimensions of our lives, yet we rarely share our faith or beliefs. This small community that gathers for theological reflection encourages us to put into words unformed thoughts and feelings about God. It gives us space and permission to voice our doubts and questions, drawing us to live our lives against a backdrop of God's continuous, loving presence. Asking questions about where God is at work in our life strengthens our relationship with God and with one another. The group itself manifests God's spirit of love. In worship, we hear about being the body of Christ, but in this small group, we *become* the body of Christ as we suffer together, celebrate together, eat and drink and grow together. Typically, this kind of conversation takes place in very few places, either in our private lives or in congregational life. And surely congregations should be the primary location for these spiritual and faithful conversations.

Another layer of belonging is added through the spiritual discipline of prayer that deeply enriches people's lives. Personal prayer in preparation for a "Reflecting with God" presentation, as well as prayer at the beginning and end of each meeting, deepens a sense of intimate conversation with God. Also, group members form bonds that make praying for one another seem natural. People who have not previously incorporated prayer into their lives find that prayer comes naturally as they give voice to hopes and concerns for group members. Talking with others about God helps us to see that God is close and intimately involved in our lives. Prayer seems a natural outflow of that conversation, a comfortable way of chatting with God, who becomes friend rather than distant relative.

I believe that people hunger to form a close relationship with God and to have a sense of belonging to God both personally and communally. Through this small group as a microcosm of a faith community, belonging to God and one another takes on flesh and becomes a living experience.

Worship Transformed

Worship offers an opportunity to gather up the joys and concerns of the people of God. Worship is a time for theological reflection as a communal event. As a parish pastor, I found that the purpose and preparation of worship changed when I was involved with theological reflection groups. First, I got to know people very well as we shared life experiences and faith conversations. Pastoral relationships took on depth and intimacy. Also, I was much more aware of the kinds of spiritual and theological questions people carried in their hearts. I became acquainted with individual spiritual needs and gained a greater sense of the congregation as a whole. And I learned that there was much more diversity within the congregation than I had first assumed. For convenience, most of us describe congregations using labels such as "conservative" or "liberal" or "evangelical." I have found that these labels are not useful in identifying the spectrum of theologies present in any given congregation.

I learned that I did not know very much about very much. When I listened to people describing their lives and offering theological reflection presentations about issues they were dealing with, I was being invited into their lives, invited beyond the borders of polite conversation. Rather than getting a superficial view of people from their actions, I learned why people made certain decisions or took particular actions. This experience reminds me of a saying from my family: "We judge ourselves by our intentions. We judge others by their actions." I felt that I had moved to hearing people's intentions, as well as their hopes, fears, and longings.

I heard about the personal, community, and political pressures on teachers, nurses, doctors, technicians, sanitary workers, scientists, academics, real estate agents, laborers, homemakers, managers, unemployed workers, students, social workers, mothers, librarians, fathers, accountants, and children. I knew nothing about these lives except superficially and from making assumptions, but I needed to know everything I could to plan and lead worship that truly gathered this community of faithful people. I learned a great deal more about education, health care, economics, and business systems from listening to congregation members who were steeped in these contexts. I learned more from my members than I did from news reports or from denominational reports and documents. In addition, I learned that people's lives are complex, whether that complexity comes from being pulled in many directions or from dealing with a single issue, such as poor health or poverty.

All this learning has changed the way I understand the community of faith. Rather than seeing the faith community as a place where people come to be fed by a minister with theological answers, I began to see it as a place where we all need to be theologians. We need to share our contextual wisdom with one another, reflect theologically on issues arising from our contexts, give space for faith exploration, offer support at times of doubt and crisis, and celebrate together as often as possible. I am one theologian among many. We all need to reflect theologically as individuals and as a community.

In worship planning, I asked myself, "How I can support the vocational life of the congregation in this service?" Not being a very visual-minded person myself, I worked hard to include visual signs and symbols of people's lives apart from the church building. I wanted to demonstrate that these lives expressed God's Holy Spirit. For example, before a Labor Day service, I invited people to bring symbols of their work to worship so that we could see the tools of our labor. We could see a laptop computer, a stethoscope, books, plumbing and carpentry tools, a calculator and a plant, among other things. These tools were placed on the communion table so that there was a physical and spiritual connection to the act of eating and drinking together in remembrance of Jesus Christ. The sermon reflected on work, whether in the home, outside the home, or in the community; whether volunteer or paid. We reflected on work that brings satisfaction, work that alienates, and the pressure of seeking work. People felt a sense of affirmation that they worked in partnership with God, with tools consecrated for God's work. Some had never considered that the work they did could be their vocation. In thinking about the concept of vocation, people acknowledged a deeper sense of purpose and meaning in their lives.

Building on this sense of meaning and purpose, as well as working at offering visual symbols, I planned one service to affirm our baptism, on the feast of the Baptism of Jesus. Using an idea from a church-school resource, I purchased several hundred small, clear, glass pebbles from an arts-and-crafts store. I placed these pebbles in the baptismal font and added water. The pebbles were almost invisible. I preached briefly on our baptism as a ritual that embodies God's grace freely given, saying that through our baptism we are called to commit our lives in service to God. I invited people to come to the font, dip their hands in the water, make a sign of the cross on their forehead with the water and say, "I remember my baptism and I am glad," an adaptation of Martin Luther's confession of faith.

I also invited people to take one of the pebbles as a visible sign of God's invisible grace. I expected that the ritual would take approximately 15 minutes, about the same length of time it would take to serve communion to the 200 people present. The organist was prepared to play some gentle music, baptismal hymns that people might quietly hum or sing. I was not prepared for the 40 minutes it took for people to engage in what was a moving and life-changing experience. Fortunately, the organist capably continued to play music throughout this liturgy. Families stood together at the font, drawing signs of the cross on each other's foreheads. Individuals wept as they touched the water and renewed their baptismal vows. People did not hurry; they took time to stay in the moment, experiencing deep feelings unlocked in a simple ritual. I was further amazed that people kept those pebbles. About a year later, when I ran into a congregation member in the supermarket, he got out his wallet and showed me his pebble. He said every time he dug into his wallet, he was reminded that God was with him, calling him to careful stewardship. A woman showed me her pebble, which she carried in her purse to remind her that through her baptism she was God's servant. These theologians astounded me with their faith.

In another service, affectionately called the "defoliation service," I invited all the children to join me in pruning a hugely overgrown five-foot shrub from the church parlor. We cut the shrub to a one-foot stump with a few leaves left. From the greenery that had been removed we took the tips to plant in pots that were available for people to take home and tend. Muddy and surrounded by our stumpy shrub and lots of little cuttings, we reflected on situations that cut us down, such as death, unemployment, and mental illness. We talked about where we find support to carry on. In the case of the plants, it was soil, water, light, and love. For us, it was family and friends and a faith community who listen to and support us, people who can be faithful for us when we are reduced to a stump.

After a couple of months, we brought the stumpy shrub and several of the cuttings into worship. New life and growth were clearly evident. Beautiful, vibrant green shoots were a delight to behold. We saw shoots springing forth from a seemingly dead stump. We celebrated this new life, as well as our faith in the possibility of new life even when we cannot see it clearly in the immediate moment.

Along with these visual services, I tried to write prayers that reflected the everyday realities of people's lives, praying for particular professions and types of work, being attentive to both joys and tensions in this work. Getting to know members more intimately through theological reflection meant that prayers were more real and relevant. God was close rather than distant, personal rather than a concept. God was part of people's joys and struggles.

Many congregations include "the prayers of the people" or other such communal prayers in their worship services. Often these prayers are offered by congregation members rather than by the minister so that the prayers are close to the daily concerns of family, work and community life. This is a wonderful idea, as long as people have thought about the ministry offered within these prayers. In my experience, these prayers seem just as formulaic and remote as most ministers' prayers. For me, communal prayer is a time to talk to God about the lives we lead, a time to celebrate and communicate with the incarnate God in our midst. God may be transcendent, a distant relative we visit once in a while, but God is also within us and within the neighbors next to us on the pews and in the world. This particular time of prayer is an opportunity to make a strong connection between our faith and our life.

Another area of worship life affected by our theological reflection groups was the annual covenanting service. I inherited a service that focused on a Sunday school rally in early fall. I wanted to take seriously the important covenantal commitment of Sunday school teachers and children. In addition, I wanted to affirm the commitment of the congregation as a whole. Covenanting with the church school alone did not do justice to God's covenant as a call to all creation. This covenant is bigger than church school, bigger than our immediate congregation. It embraces the whole world. After discussion in both the church school and worship committees, we changed this covenanting service to focus on the covenant between God and our whole congregation. We celebrated and recommitted ourselves, not just to church life, but also to family life, work life, and community life. Placing the work of church school in the context of a whole-life commitment actually gave more emphasis to the Christian education enterprise. Christian education did not stand alone, a practice that previously had been thought to give it visibility and make it easier to "recruit" church-school teachers. Instead, Christian education became part of a whole vision of a committed Christian life. Because people in the congregation had been reflecting theologically, they had a stronger sense of God's call on their whole lives. They wanted worship that resonated with that call.

While listening to the rich faith lives and theological questions that were shared in theological reflection groups, I began to wish that this wisdom could be shared more broadly. With this thought in mind, I offered a seminar on how to preach. A small group of people responded to this invitation—people who already brought considerable skills as writers, speakers, and teachers. What they needed was to understand how to write and offer a sermon. After meeting for a number of weeks to think about sermons, to examine sermon-writing resources such as commentaries, and to share practice sermons, these people were inspired to preach. At various points in the church year, we heard from these committed congregational members about personal, political, and social issues with a powerful theological connection. For instance, with wisdom and compassion, Bill preached about gambling from his perspective of community work. His community association had been raising

102 Reflecting with God

102 *Reflecting with God*

102 — *Reflecting with God*

funds for all kinds of worthy causes through charitable bingo games, where people in the lowest income category bring their hopes for instant riches. Through theological reflection he offered a great deal for us to consider about the ways gambling affects people's lives. Preaching from within our faith community was, and still is, an opportunity to hear about the living word of God at work in the world. Hearing from these preachers gave richness to the liturgical year, as we listened to multiple voices offering experiences and insights about God and faith. It also strengthened a sense that we are a community of theologians.

As a congregational leader, I learned much about the faith community, worship, pastoral care, spiritual nurture, and leadership as I participated in theological reflection with congregation members. I learned more about the everyday struggles in people's lives in an environment where we were trying to talk with one another about our faith and how God was at work. The concept of ministry became a lived experience rather than an intellectual notion.

Ministry of a Whole People

A great deal has been written about the ministry of the laity. Many books included in the annotated bibliography explore this topic in depth. While many ministers preach and talk about ministry of the laity, this concept does not seem to produce the hoped-for revolutionary change of congregational life or people's personal lives. In my own denomination, we talk about the "whole people of God," yet hierarchy, bureaucracy, and an elevated understanding of ordination undermine the concept that God calls all to ministry. Most laypeople do not have a clear sense of vocation or ministry, or an ability to talk about their faith as connected to their life. They find it hard to connect their daily lives to their faith. Those who do feel a sense of call assume that call is to "The Ministry," meaning ordination. I believe that if we had a more vital sense of the ministry of the whole people, people would understand that ministry is about more than ordination. At workshops on ministry of the laity, I ask people to discuss how gifts of ministry are celebrated and held accountable in their congregation and how celebration and accountability could be created. This exercise illustrates that we need to take deliberate steps to create ways to talk about ministry as something in which we all participate. It is more than a nice concept to preach about on Sunday morning; it needs to be lived daily in the lives of individuals and in the entire life of the congregation.

After several years of conducting theological reflection groups, I found that through this process people made a stronger connection between their daily lives and their faith. People became more confident about using theological language to describe their experiences. They began to see themselves as ministers and theologians. People affirmed one another in their ministries. As I have watched people grow in their understanding that they are ministers, I have also begun to wonder whether using the term "ministry of the laity" creates a barrier. In most people's minds there is a hierarchy beginning with ordained ministry, moving down toward lay ministry, a situation of first- and second-class citizenship in God's kingdom. If we are all called by God, if we are all theologians, then distinctions between lay and ordained ministry are not necessary.

Working with students who hope to be ordained ministers, I hear them struggle to understand what it means to be a congregational leader. Cathy worried about her sense of pastoral identity as a leader. "People will look to me as their minister to have all the answers," she declared. I asked her if she knew such a minister, this paragon who had all the answers. Evidently, there are a few who do believe that they have answers. However, most ministers I know understand that effective ministry is being present and asking questions that will encourage theological reflection. As her confidence grew, Cathy began to understand this concept.

Supporting the ministry of the whole people is essential to a healthy congregation. As a leader, I learned that all-important skill—when to get out of people's way. Staying focused on a vision that we are a community of theologians and ministers, I schooled myself in language that would encourage others. For instance, Sadie came to tell me that Joan was back in the hospital. I thanked her for letting me know and asked her to say "Hi" to Joan when she visited. While she, and others with whom I used this response, were taken aback, they quickly realized that we care for one another as a community. I was not the proxy visitor. In addition, I was not the proxy praying person. Rather than praying at community gatherings, I encouraged and taught others how to pray. Initially, people were shocked when I said no to an invitation to pray at a communal gathering. Yet people quickly grasped that we were a community of praying people, not a community led by one praying representative. When people came to me with ideas for projects in the congregation or in the community, I expressed delight and said that I looked forward to seeing how it turned out. Again, people were surprised because they thought they were presenting an idea to me that I was supposed to bring to fruition. After the surprise, people got on with the project and discovered their own gifts for ministry. In getting out of people's way, we were truly a community of theologians and ministers.

God is intimately involved in our lives, giving them meaning and purpose. We can look for God in the computer screen we face each day, in company meetings, and in our teaching and healing. With clear support from our faith community as a place where theological conversation takes place, we can maintain a sense of God's presence in all areas of our lives. Theological reflection offers one way to focus that theological conversation.

Learning to See God

Engaging in theological reflection with congregation members reminds me that as a community of faith, we need to stay focused about developing our faith and spirituality. In the busyness of congregational life we can lose track of the reason that we gather as a community. We are not a social club; we are gathered as a people of God to be sent forth in service to God. Being gathered, we hear and experience a relationship with God through the faith community. Being sent forth, we are dispersed to live our faith and to experience God at work in the world. Theological reflection is one spiritual discipline that helps us to make a connection between being gathered and being sent forth.

Whether you are doing theological reflection within a group or individually, it is one of a number of spiritual disciplines such as prayer, fasting, tithing, or offering hospitality. Spiritual disciplines have been part of the practices of faithful men, women, and communities for centuries through monasteries, hermitages, and convents. In addition, ordinary Christians have practiced spiritual disciplines. There is Margaret, who reads the Bible as part of her daily routine. A faithful group gathers each Friday to offer prayer for congregation members. Monica fasts in solidarity with those who go hungry, to remind herself of her privileged life. Jenna and Frank practice hospitality in opening their home to people in need. Few of us can offer our entire lives to rigorous religious spirituality; however, we can live our lives as faithfully as possible.

Maintaining a conscious sense of God's presence in our lives is difficult, especially when we live and work without any explicit reference to God. In our workplaces and in our family activities, we rarely mention God unless we have become mindful or disciplined about recognizing God's presence in our lives. Some families make a point of praying before a meal or at the end of a day before bedtime. Some individuals make a point of a daily quiet time for prayer and meditation. But few of us work in places where prayer or conversation about faith and God can take place. And in some environments, prayer or talk of God would not be allowed, either because we tend to separate the private practice of faith from a public work environment, or because we want to respect the faith practices of others in a multifaith context. Most people have little time to practice spiritual disciplines and spend most of their time in an explicitly secular context.

Being aware of God's spirit at work in our lives is challenging and requires being disciplined about our spiritual lives. Spiritual disciplines have two components: understanding that there is more to our lives than what we see directly in front of us, and deliberately seeking to connect with God. Understanding that there is more to our lives than the daily tasks before us gives us a broader perspective, a sense of purpose and satisfaction that comes from serving God. Rather than dividing the world into a concrete, earthly realm and a spiritual realm, I prefer to believe that we are called to love God with all our hearts, minds, and bodies, and that the spiritual is deeply embedded within our earthly lives. However, using the term *spiritual* reminds us that our life is cherished by God and that we are called by God to be in relationship with others. We are called out of our daily routines and concerns to a greater awareness of God and others. I am reminded of this call when my partner and I have an opportunity to go out to dinner. We do communicate with each other on a daily basis, checking out schedules, meals, and who needs to go where. But when we are sitting across from each other over a relaxed meal, we find that our conversation moves to another level. We move beyond daily maintenance to what is in our hearts, what ideas are percolating, what frustrations and aspirations are below the surface. We talk about what gives us meaning and purpose and hope, topics at the heart of our being that nurture our spirit. In this way we connect with one another spiritually. Being more aware of the presence of God deepens and strengthens our faith, and the spiritual discipline of theological reflection is one way to experience God's presence.

The second aspect of spiritual discipline is intention. This is the part most people shy away from, because discipline is not always welcome; it is hard work. Yet it takes discipline to maintain a program of health, whether that is physical exercise or spiritual exercise. I worked for 10 years as a professional violinist. Despite hours of playing all day, I woke up each morning facing the necessary discipline of practice. Muscles and reflexes needed to be strong and finely toned. Much of the time my passion for playing the violin made it easy for me to be disciplined. However, there were many days when it was hard work to open the violin case and persuade reluctant fingers to go through the series of exercises that would prepare me for taking part in strenuous rehearsals and learning new pieces of music.

Just as doing warm-up exercises and practicing pieces to be performed are necessary to the life of a violinist, spiritual disciplines are essential to the life of a Christian. Taking time to be with God, to be aware of God's presence in our lives, nurtures our spiritual life. Our passion to be in relationship with God and the positive impact of God's presence in our lives keeps us motivated. However, maintaining a connection with God can be hard work. It requires commitment, purpose, and intention.

Some of us are more organized and disciplined than others, and each of us needs to find ways to stimulate our discipline. As a violinist, having a lesson with a teacher or rehearsing with a group of musicians or preparing for a concert gave me impetus to maintain my daily routine of practicing. Similarly, maintaining a faithful Christian discipline is easier when we meet with a spiritual mentor or a small group to whom we are accountable, when we spend time with people who will encourage a life of faith. Knowing I am accountable to a group of people supports my resolve to reflect theologically as a spiritual discipline. And by doing so on a regular basis, I maintain my connection with God more easily. My hope in doing theological reflection is that reflecting with God on our daily lives becomes second nature, a habit of the heart.

God's Call, Our Response

One theological reflection group wrestled with the question of seeing God's presence. Where can they see God at work in their lives? They agreed that they were not expecting to see a burning bush or to hear a booming voice from the sky. Yet within the ordinary task of tending sheep, Moses had an extraordinary experience of God. A burning bush described that encounter with God. The group decided that a burning bush was not a literal event but a metaphor for times when they did experience or identify God in their lives. For instance, Anne works with noncommunicative children, using a "facilitated board," a method that enables a trusted adult to help a child communicate by writing. She began to see that "when my student said on his facilitated board that he does not like being autistic, that's a burning bush right there. I mean, it's really amazing for a noncommunicative person to have that little burst of communicating with you; it is truly a burning bush." From being an extraordinary image of God's presence outside people's experience, the burning bush became a metaphor for sighting the extraordinary within ordinary events of life.

As confidence in seeking and finding God increases, faith conversation becomes a normal part of congregational life. In many denominations, congregation members feel comfortable witnessing to their faith, yet many more congregations are uncomfortable with this kind of faith conversation. In small groups, people are encouraged to talk about their faith. Theological language becomes part of their vocabulary. And these conversations spill over into the larger life of the congregation. I found that people were asking questions in committees about where God was present. When making decisions about the use of the church building and financial directions, people were asking whether we were fulfilling God's call. Christian education committees were wondering how children could make a stronger connection between the biblical story and their lives of faith. Theological questions were becoming part of people's vocabulary and consequently part of church structures.

While we hear the words and may even believe that God's call to humanity is personal and individual, we may not feel that the call includes us as individuals. As I mentioned earlier, seeing God at work in others is far easier than seeing God and feeling God at work in our own lives. Yet if we believe God calls each one of us, we might also believe that God is interested in our particular life. Believing that, we respond by looking for God, by putting on lenses that help us see God's handprint in our lives, by listening for God's spirit in those around us. When we share with others in this search for God, whether with a personal mentor or a small group, we develop more skill and confidence in seeking and finding God. When others point to an incident whereby they see God's spirit in our lives, we experience a powerful epiphany.

Theological reflection encourages us to see God in our lives, because the process assumes that God is at work among us. We assume God's presence, and we go searching for signs of that presence. God's presence may seem obvious, yet most good Christians feel a gap between their belief in God and their sense of God's presence in their lives. God's activity as creator occurs on a grand scale, encompassing universes, stars, moon and sun, seas, and whole worlds. So what does God have to do with me? Our daily routines feel far removed from the concerns of God—concerns that include tides of history, social justice for oppressed peoples, and care of the environment. Yet God's grand works are accomplished only through an intimate knowledge of the tiniest parts of the universe. God is not only creator of many universes; God continues to be in relationship with creation on a molecular level as well as a universal scale. God turns the tides of history one human being at a time, so we need to take seriously God's call to relationship with creation and all creatures, including us. With the possibility before us for a closer relationship with God and a richer life of faith, my question is, Why would we *not* want to reflect theologically?

Appendix

SESSION 1: INTRODUCTION

- Welcome people and do icebreaker exercise or opening.
- Develop a group covenant.
- Describe the process.
- Set dates and times of all sessions.
- Set schedule of theological reflection presentations.
- Hand out "Reflecting with God."
- End with wrap-up.
- Close with prayer, meditation, or poem.

SESSION 2: INTRODUCTION

- Open with prayer, meditation, or poem.
- "Check in" with one another.
- Revisit and establish group covenant.
- Get to know one another: pattern of a typical day.
- End with wrap-up.
- Close with prayer, meditation, or poem.

SUBSEQUENT SESSIONS:
THEOLOGICAL REFLECTION PRESENTATIONS

Each person in the group is assigned a meeting at which he or she will present a theological reflection, followed by group discussion.

GROUP PROCESS	APPROXIMATE TIMES
• Opening prayer, meditation, or poem	10 minutes
• Check-in	15 minutes
• Presentation of theological reflection	15 minutes
• Break	10 minutes
• Group discussion	50 minutes
• Wrap-up	10 minutes
• Closing prayer, meditation, or poem	10 minutes

LAST SESSION: SAYING GOODBYE

- Evaluation of time together
- Refreshments or meal
- Closing rituals

Reflecting with God

1. Naming the Experience: *Choosing an Event on Which to Reflect*

Choose an event, a moment, a conversation, or a situation. As you recall the event, ask yourself:
- What happened?
- Who was involved?
- What did you do or say?

2. Exploring the Experience: *Finding Another Layer to the Event*

To explore another layer in this event, ask yourself:
- How did you feel?
- What challenged, stimulated, or disturbed you?
- What was happening for others in the situation?

3. Digging Deeper: *Expanding Your Thinking*

To discover another layer of reflection, ask yourself:
- What do you think about the situation?
- What core values emerge as you think about this event?
- What values are different from yours?
- What social issues, power issues, or economic issues are at work?

4. Making Faith Connections: *Finding God at Work in This Event*

To make faith connections, ask yourself:
- Where is God present for you in this situation?
- Where is God present for others?
- Does this event remind you of a Scripture passage, a hymn, or other resources from your faith tradition?
- What theological issues or themes are present?
- What traditions of our church speak to this situation?
- Are you affirmed or challenged in your present actions or beliefs?

5. Learning: *Naming Your Discoveries*

To draw out what you learned, ask yourself:
- What questions still linger?
- Were you challenged to change present actions or beliefs?
- What have you learned about yourself?
- What have you learned about God?
- What do you need?
- What will you do now?

6. Praying: *Taking Time with God*

To conclude your reflection, write a prayer emerging from this event.

7. Presenting to the Group: *Preparing for Group Discussion*

Present your written reflection to the group by reading it aloud. This reading will be followed by group discussion. As you think about the discussion time, how would you like the group to focus? Discussion is not a problem-solving exercise but a way to extend your personal reflection. Here are some suggestions to focus the group discussion:
- Is there a question still lingering for which you would like group wisdom?
- Do you want group members to share their experiences with a similar situation?
- Do you want to hear group members' thoughts about further theological or biblical connections?
- Do you want to know where others see God at work?

Bibliography

Congregational Life

Adams, James, and Celia Hahn. *Learning To Share the Ministry: A Minister's Sabbatical as an Experiment.* Washington, D.C.: Alban Institute, 1985.

Through a minister's sabbatical experience, the congregation of St. Mark's has an opportunity to examine issues of power and communication between lay and ordered ministry within the institutional church.

Crabtree, Davida F. *The Empowering Church: How One Congregation Supports Lay People's Ministries in the World.* Washington, D.C.: Alban Institute, 1989.

Crabtree's doctor of ministry thesis documents her work with Colchester Federated Church as the congregation grapples personally and corporately with the importance of understanding the ministry of all God's people, focused on people's ministry outside the institutional church.

Diehl, William E. *Christianity and Real Life.* Philadelphia: Fortress, 1985.

An exploration of the failure of the church to affirm and support the ministry of the laity in the workplace.

————. *In Search of Faithfulness: Lessons from the Christian Community.* Philadelphia: Fortress, 1987, 1989.

Diehl uses the framework of Thomas J. Peters and Robert H. Waterman from their book *In Search of Excellence* to understand Christian discipleship in many areas, such as a search for identity; a quest for growth in faith; a need for community; and justice in the world. Written by a business executive in the language of business, it is an excellent exploration of ministry.

————. *Thank God It's Monday.* Philadelphia: Fortress, 1982.

Looking at societal power, Diehl articulates a theology for a competitive society, providing a biblical base and challenging the institutional church to liberate the laity.

————. *Ministry in Daily Life: A Practical Guide for Congregations.* Bethesda, Md.: Alban Institute, 1996.

Full of practical experience and wisdom, this book demonstrates specific ways to affirm, equip and support members.

————. *The Monday Connection.* San Francisco: HarperSanFrancisco, 1991.

Diehl explores the connections between faith and daily life, with their implications for laity. He focuses on the call to ministry of all God's people through a ministry of competence, presence, ethics, change, and lifestyle.

Hahn, Celia. *Lay Voices in an Open Church.* Washington, D.C.: Alban Institute, 1985.

Hahn raises radical and important questions about the nature of church in the lives of laypeople.

Hawkins, Thomas R. *The Learning Congregation: A New Vision of Leadership.* Louisville: Westminster John Knox, 1997.

Hawkins proposes a fresh and highly practical approach to congregational leadership, providing practical strategies for understanding the relationship between leadership, learning, and ministry.

Leas, Speed B., and Roy M. Oswald. *The Inviting Church: A Study of New Member Assimilation.* Washington, D.C.: Alban Institute, 1987.

By looking at church growth factors, church size, and how to attract and recruit new members, Leas and Oswald explore ways to be an inviting congregation.

Phillips, Roy D. *Letting Go: Transforming Congregations for Ministry.* Bethesda, Md.: Alban Institute, 2002.

For lay ministries to flourish, pastors need to let go of their traditional views about their role in the congregation.

Whitehead, James D., and Evelyn Eaton Whitehead. *Community of Faith: Models and Strategies for Developing Christian Communities.* New York: Seabury, 1982. New edition: *Community of Faith: Crafting Christian Communities Today.* Mystic, Conn.: Twenty-Third Publications, 1992.

Using newer information about group process, the Whiteheads reflect on the components of Christian community, as well as on the purpose of and the way to be an actively engaged community.

———. *The Promise of Partnership: Leadership and Ministry in an Adult Church.* San Francisco: HarperSanFrancisco, 1991.

Beginning with ministry as a response to God's call in the lives of all people, the Whiteheads explore a model of partnership in ministry.

Spirituality and Theology

Bass, Dorothy C., ed. *Practicing Our Faith: A Way of Life for a Searching People.* San Francisco: Jossey-Bass, 1997.

An exploration of 12 central Christian faith practices offers insight into personal and communal spirituality. Practices such as keeping the Sabbath and forgiving one another demonstrate shared activities that address fundamental human needs and form a way of life.

Brizee, Robert. *Where in the World Is God?* Nashville: Upper Room, 1987.

Using stories from daily life, Brizee offers ways to point to the activity of God in small and large decisions as well as in everyday life.

Brooke, Avery. *Finding God in the World: Reflections on a Spiritual Journey.* San Francisco: Harper & Row, 1989.

An autobiography of Brooke's spiritual journey from agnosticism to spiritual director offers reflections on her awakening to the presence of God in all of her life, an immanent spirituality that engages the world, and ways of staying connected with the biblical story.

Day-Lower, Donna C., and John Raines. *Modern Work and Human Meaning.* Philadelphia: Westminster, 1986.

Using the real-life situations of the unemployed, this book examines the meaning and alienation of work and joblessness.

Jacobsen, Steve. *Hearts to God, Hands to Work: Connecting Spirituality and Work.* Bethesda, Md.: Alban Institute, 1997.

For pastors who want to understand laity as ministers, Jacobsen offers insights into understanding the connection between faith and daily work.

Rowthorn, Anne. *The Liberation of the Laity.* Wilton, Conn.: Morehouse-Barlow, 1986.

Using feminist and liberation theologies, Rowthorn suggests a naming and reclaiming of the ministry of the laity. Writing in revolutionary language, Rowthorn stirs the hearts of laity.

Soelle, Dorothy, with Shirley A. Cloyes. *To Work and to Love: A Theology of Creation.* Philadelphia: Fortress, 1984.

Soelle explores foundations for ministry through an exploration of the spirituality of work, from the biblical perspective of being created in God's image and being called as "co-creators."

Small-Group Ministry

Bushman, John H., and Sandy Jones. *Developing the Art of Discussion: Handbook for Use with Church Groups.* Philadelphia: Judson, 1977.

Bushman and Jones offer a hands-on approach to small-group discussion. Topics cover getting acquainted, establishing trust, taking responsibility to participate, listening in groups, assuming roles in groups, and engaging in extended discussion.

Costa, Donna M. *The Ministry of God's People.* Nashville: [United Methodist] Discipleship Resources, 1991.

An excellent resource book for small-group study exploring how people can articulate a sense of call and discernment of gifts for ministry. Continuing the theme of call, Costa suggests Christian growth is an unfolding call: to servanthood, to grace, and to covenant.

Dozier, Verna. *The Authority of the Laity.* Washington, D.C.: Alban Institute, 1982.

Exploring from the Old Testament to the New Testament, Dozier calls people to a new reformation rather than an abdication of their authority as ministers.

Dozier, Verna; Celia Hahn; and Patricia Drake. *The Authority of the Laity: A Study Guide.* Washington, D.C.: Alban Institute,1983.

————. *The Calling of the Laity.* Washington, D.C.: Alban Institute, 1988.

A wonderful collection of writings by laypeople about "front-line" ministry in the workplace.

————. *The Dream of God: A Call to Return.* Boston: Cowley Publications, 1991.

Dozier offers a prophetic recollection of our call to follow Jesus and not merely to worship him.

————. *Equipping the Saints: A Method of Self-directed Bible Study for Lay Groups.* Washington, D.C.: Alban Institute, 1981.

Dozier briefly outlines a method of questions for Bible study and discussion, providing examples of how one group worked at its study.

Eppley, Harold Webb, and Rochelle Yolanda Melander, eds. *Starting Small Groups and Keeping Them Going.* Minneapolis: Augsburg Fortress, 1995.

If you are interested in starting a small-group ministry, this book offers useful approaches to organization and development as well as to the training of facilitators.

Farnham, Suzanne G.; Joseph P. Gill; R. Taylor McLean; and Susan M. Ward. *Listening Hearts: Discerning Call in Community.* Philadelphia: Morehouse, 1991.

Using a variety of spiritual disciplines, the authors present a process for individuals and groups to explore discernment of call and gifts for ministry.

Grenz, Linda L., and J. Fletcher Lowe, Jr. *Ministry in Daily Life: A Guide to the Baptismal Covenant.* New York: Episcopal Church, 1996.

Grenz and Lowe offer a useful resource to develop and enhance understandings of a ministry in daily life.

Oswald, Roy M., with Jackie McMakin. *How to Prevent Lay Leader Burnout.* Washington, D.C.: Alban Institute, 1984.

An excellent resource that looks at the care of lay leadership within the institutional church.

Peel, Donald. *The Ministry of the Laity: Sharing the Leadership, Sharing the Task.* Toronto: Anglican Book Centre, 1991.

A "how to" book for groups to explore a ministry of the laity from the point of view of both voluntarism within the institutional church, in particular in an Anglican polity, and the understanding of ministry in the workplace.

Reber, Robert. *Linking Faith and Daily Life: An Educational Program for Lay People.* Washington, D.C.: Alban Institute, 1991.

A culmination of a three-year project, this program provides a process for laypeople to explore their faith and its connections to all facets of life. This is a detailed program workbook for small-group ministry.

Saunders, Clark, and Clair Woodbury. *Ministry as an Art: Exploring Volunteer and Professional Church Leadership.* Toronto: United Church Publishing House, 1996.

Part 1 explores the public arts of worship, pastoral care, and leadership. Part 2 looks at the arts of innovation, encouragement, conflict management, education, giving, and social action.

Williams, Ronald C. *Serving God with Style: Unleashing Servant Potential.* Bethesda, Md.: Alban Institute, 2002.

A tool for training ministry volunteers, called a "faith-style inventory," useful for developing ministry teams, ministry leaders, and a Christ-centered work ethic; and for empowering Christians in a secular workplace.

Wingeier, Douglas E. *Eight Ways to Become a Christian: Sharing Your Story of Faith.* Nashville: [United Methodist] Discipleship Resources, 1988.

Through the written faith stories of eight people, Wingeier encourages others to articulate and share their own faith stories with each other.

————. *New Testament Images of Learning at Seven Life Stages.* Nashville: Discipleship Resources, 1982.

Using Scripture and biblical images, Wingeier looks at the ways we learn. The accompanying discussion questions encourage an individual reader or group members to explore their own learning and the learning of others in the congregation.

―――. *Working Out Your Own Beliefs: A Guide for Doing Your Own Theology*. Auckland, New Zealand: College Communications, 1986.

Concerned about the gap people feel between faith and daily life, Wingeier uses experience, Scripture, tradition, and reason to show how people can develop their own theology.

Conflict

Hobgood, William Chris. *Welcoming Resistance: A Path to Faithful Ministry*. Bethesda: Alban, 2001.

Although it may be tempting to believe that battles have been won when resistance is gone, it is amid the give-and-take of change initiators and resisters interacting openly and with mutual respect that congregations become lively and richer places.

Leas, Speed B. *Discover Your Conflict Management Style*. Revised Edition. Bethesda: Alban Institute, 1997.

Leas offers a tool to assess your innate conflict style as well as to explore a variety of options appropriate to different levels of conflict.

Lott, David B., ed. *Conflict Management in Congregations*. Bethesda: Alban Institute, 2001.

This gathering of 20 classic works on congregational conflict features Speed Leas, George Parsons, Margaret Bruehl, Gil Rendle, and others, who look at various approaches to conflict management.

Rendle, Gil. *Behavioral Covenants in Congregations: A Handbook for Honoring Differences*. Bethesda: Alban Institute, 2001.

Addressing the issue of uncivil behavior in congregations, Rendle offers a handbook on how to live creatively together by valuing our differences rather than trying to ignore or blend them.

Theological Reflection

Killen, Patricia O'Connell, and John de Beer. *The Art of Theological Reflection*. New York: Crossroads, 1994.

This clearly written book offers concrete, creative, and flexible ways to make connections between life experiences and faith for individuals, small groups, and faith communities. Following a theoretical exploration of theological reflection, the authors offer a variety of methods for the reflective process and include a final chapter on how to create a theological reflection process in the midst of pastoral practice.

Faith and Work

Kowalski, Judith A., and Dean J. Collins. *To Serve and Protect: Law Enforcement Officers Reflect on Their Faith and Work*. Minneapolis: Augsburg, 1992.

Through interviews with people working in law enforcement, the authors express principles of healthy spirituality: helping others, seeking justice and truth, protecting people from harm, upholding right, stopping violence, and peacefully intervening in criminal situations.

Palmer, Parker. *The Active Life: A Spirituality of Work, Creativity and Caring*. San Francisco: Harper & Row, 1990.

This book explores the question "What kind of spirituality works for busy, active 20th century people?" For those struggling to find the link between busyness and purpose, Palmer offers insights and personal stories.

Peck, George, and John S. Hoffman, eds. *The Laity in Ministry: The Whole People of God for the Whole World*. Valley Forge: Judson, 1984.

A number of writers critically reflect on a concept of ministry of the laity, providing case studies of people making connections between work and faith.

Pierce, Gregory F. Augustine, ed. *Of Human Hands: A Reader in the Spirituality of Work.* Minneapolis: Augsburg. 1991.

Read this collection to glimpse various perspectives on a ministry of the laity.

Slattery, Patrick, ed. *Caretakers of Creation: Farmers Reflect on Their Faith and Work.* Minneapolis: Augsburg/ACTA, 1991.

Nine farmers describe their ministry of farming, focusing on a commitment to the stewardship of creation.

Sorensen, David Allen, and Barbara Degrote-Sorensen. *Kindling the Spark: A Dialogue with Christian Teachers on Their Work.* Chicago: ACTA, 1992.

One of a series of four books that look directly at the work of laity. This book reflects on a number of areas in the lives of teachers, including motivation, relationships, burnout, balance, and moments of inspiration.